Mediatization of Public Se

Thomas Schillemans

Mediatization of Public Services

How Organizations Adapt to News Media

PETER LANG

Frankfurt am Main · Berlin · Bern · Bruxelles · New York · Oxford · Wien

Bibliographic Information published by the Deutsche Nationalbibliothek
The Deutsche Nationalbibliothek lists this publication in the Deutsche Nationalbibliografie; detailed bibliographic data is available in the internet at http://dnb.d-nb.de.

Cover Design:
© Olaf Gloeckler, Atelier Platen, Friedberg

ISBN 978-3-631-63730-2

© Peter Lang GmbH
Internationaler Verlag der Wissenschaften
Frankfurt am Main 2012
All rights reserved.

www.peterlang.de

Contents

Preface 9

1. Public services and news media 11
    1.1 Public service providers 12
    1.2 Mediatization... 15
    1.3 The plan of the book... 18
    1.4 Researching mediatization 19

2. Public services... 25
    2.1 A diversity of public service providers 26
    2.2 Public service provision in Australia and the Netherlands.............. 33
    2.3 Tensions in public service provision... 35
    2.4 Conclusion 39

3. Mediatization and public services... 43
    3.1 The news media as an institution 44
    3.2 Mediatization... 48
    3.3 Mediatization of organizations... 52
    3.4 Media logic 53

4. Media pressure on public service providers 59
    4.1 Substantial and dispersed media coverage 60
    4.2 Neutrality, negativity and personalization...................................... 65
    4.3 Experiences of media pressure.. 68
    4.4 Media pressure in sum... 72

5. Mediatization of organizational inputs.. 75
    5.1 'The pictures in our head' 75
    5.2 Accommodation: multiple forms of monitoring.............................. 78
    5.3 Substitution and amalgamation: signaling...................................... 80
    5.4 Mediatization of inputs in sum 85

6. Mediatization of Organizational Throughputs 87
   6.1 The shadow of the news 88
   6.2 Accommodation: "You just don't put anything, anywhere, that
       could end up in the wrong place" 91
   6.3 Amalgamation: anticipation & centralization 94
   6.4 Substitution: the daily yardstick 99
   6.5 Mediatization of throughputs in sum 101

7. Mediatization of Organizational Outputs 103
   7.1 A mediatized playing field 104
   7.2 Accommodation: in and out of the spotlights 106
   7.3 Mediatization of organizational websites 112
   7.4 Substitution & amalgamation: government by publicity 116
   7.5 Mediatization of outputs in sum 119

8. Media logic and public services 123
   8.1 Aims: making important news interesting 124
   8.2 Rules: barriers and opportunities 126
   8.3 Production logics: chances and a major hazard 133
   8.4 Media logic and public services in sum 137

9. Organizational mediatization: playing with matches 139
   9.1 Mediatization: the process in short 140
   9.2 Researching organizational mediatization: some critical
       reflections 142
   9.3 Organizational mediatization: variations 145
   9.4 Mediatization: real and imaginary risks 148
   9.5 Playing with matches 152

References 155

Appendix: Research notes 165

List of tables and figures

Tables

Table 1 Overview research questions & research methods............................ 23
Table 2: Typology of public and third sector providers of public services........ 40
Table 3: Total numbers of annual news stories for 28 Australian service
         providers 63
Table 4: Overview mediatization organizational inputs 86
Table 5: Overview mediatization organizational throughputs 102
Table 6: Overview mediatization organizational websites............................ 115
Table 7: Overview mediatization organizational outputs 120
Table 8: Media logic: aims, rules, production logics & constraints................ 138

Figures

Figure 1: Trends in reporting on service providers in quality press 61
Figure 2: Subjective perceptions of media attention 64
Figure 3: Assessments of the quality of the media..................................... 69
Figure 4: Public service providers as news consumers................................ 77
Figure 5: Importance media on organizational level 88
Figure 6: Importance media on personal level 90
Figure 7: Mediatization of policy field.. 105

Preface

Sometimes mundane things are important. This book results from a research project on media and public organizations, conducted between 2008 and 2012 in Australia and the Netherlands. Its origins, however, hark back to the years I worked for the Council for Social Development (RMO) – a public body providing independent policy-advice to the Dutch government – where I was involved in a report on *Media Logic* (2003) in the public sector. Many of the daily routines at the council did not, at the time, stand out as particularly significant. In hindsight, however, it has occurred to me that our daily routines were thoroughly mediatized, i.e. were affected by and related to the news media. For instance, we would usually discuss the news over lunch; often referred to media-incidents in our reports; took media-incidents in account when evaluating policies; calibrated the launch of our reports to the news cycle; and participated in media-training and writing courses that helped us to phrase our research-based reports in wordings that triggered journalists. We did not deliberately try to please the media or to maximize our media exposure, but we more or less instinctively learned how to bring our messages across in our mediatized policy-environment. The news was an invisible but permanent companion and left a delicate but profound imprint on our daily activities.

This book revisits these types of organizational adaptations to the news media in the public sector. It is an empirically based analysis of changing organizational routines and practices in media-saturated societies. The analysis will show that public service providers are substantially mediatized and that this development has a large impact on their daily work and services. The impact is not readily understood in either negative or positive terms; the overall picture is mixed and multi-faceted. And mediatization is not a direct effect of what journalists, editors and media corporations *do* – and might be blamed for doing – but is more properly understood as a structural development in complex systems of governance.

A large number of people have been important in the 'production process' of this book, although I am the sole author and obviously carry full responsibility for any remaining flaw or fluke. The book is based on a number of focus groups, surveys, and interviews with 90 senior practitioners and executives working for government departments, public agencies or third sector organizations. I would like to thank all of those respondents warmly for their time and enthusiasm and for painting such vivid pictures of the roles of the media in their professional lives.

I would further like to express my gratitude to the Centre for Social Impact at the Australian School of Business, University of New South Wales, for offering me the opportunity to work on this project as a visiting scholar in the second half of 2009. I would especially like to thank Peter Shergold, Anne Measday, and Christine Norgrove at CSI, Paul 't Hart for being such an effective linking pin, and Mark Bovens and Wieger Bakker for opening up the opportunity in the first place. I would further like to thank the RMO and Rienk Janssens, ANSZOG, the South Australian Productivity Commission and Michael Watts, and Esther Lefas at CSI, for vital assistance in the practical organization of focus groups. The decision to reinvigorate my media & governance research was made in my year in Tilburg, and I would like to thank Frank Hendriks, Marcel Boogers, and Wim van der Donk for, presumably inadvertently, helping me take that decision. Parts of the book have been presented at various seminars and conferences: at the Australian National University (2009), the University of New South Wales (2009), the Utrecht School of Governance (2010), the Political Studies Association's annual conference in London (2011), at the 7th Transatlantic Dialogue of ASPA/EGPA in Newark (2011), ECREA's political communication conference in Madrid (2011), and at the Journalism, Media and Communication Department of the University of Gothenburg (2012). I would like to thank all participants in those sessions, and some other colleagues, for encouragement, feedback and useful suggestions. In particular I would like to thank Rod Tiffen, Kent Asp, Monika Djerf-Pierre, Mats Ekström, Magnus Fredriksson, Karin Geuijen, Les Hems, Bengt Johansson, Susan Keen, Albert Meijer, Ank Michels, Mirko Noordegraaf, Rien Rouw, Martijn van der Steen, Peter van Aelst, Kutsal Yesilkagit, and Sandra Jacobs. I would also like to thank Sara le Cointre, Armin Djogic, Christoph Ossege, Paul den Otter, and Minou de Ruiter for their research assistance.

This book is, to the best of my knowledge, the first attempt to analyze the mediatization of organizations providing public services. The novelty of this approach speaks for its relevance to the academic community and a general audience. On a more personal level, however, the book's relevance also lies in the dear memories it embodies of the amazing, exciting and exhausting (and highly unmediatized) months I spent with Anouk, Casper and Tycho in Coogee.

1. Public services and news media

"In other words, (...) may then win the daily battles with the news media, by getting into the news as they wish, but end up losing the war, as standards of newsworthiness begin to become prime criteria to evaluate issues, policies, and politics". (Cook 2005, 163)

In the first weeks of June 2012, the Dutch media was dominated by three major issues: the lamentable state of the Dutch national football team, the probabilities of *Grexit* (Greek exit from the euro) and the early preparations for the upcoming Parliamentary elections. At first glance, the dominance of these three news issues underscores some of the key insights from political communications research. It highlights the rising importance of soft news, it underlines the unceasing importance of economic news and it displays the media's keen interest in everything that has to do with campaigns and elections. However, the observant viewer, with a disinterest in sports, could easily have been struck by a less spectacular yet politically highly significant and under-explored undercurrent in the news: daily items and television productions on organizations that provide public services. This observant viewer could for instance have watched *Border Security* or *Bondi Rescue*, both dramatized real life soaps about officials protecting the borders of New Zealand or people at the beaches in the eastern suburbs of Sydney. Should (s)he have tuned in to one of the newsreels, (s)he would have seen how different public health care organizations were subjected to critical news stories, for instance about their treatment of hernia, the provision of unnecessary hospital care, or the pro's and con's of treating mentally ill patients at home. The observant viewer would also have seen that the independent *Netherlands Bureau for Economic Policy Analysis* was publicly rebuked for its apparent undue political influence. And should (s)he have counted and analyzed all the domestic news stories in the quality press, (s)he would have found that almost a third of the news stories focused on the myriad of organizations delivering public services.

Most political communication research tunes in on the central actors in democracies, and analyses the behavior of politicians, ministers, governments or political parties; with a heavy preference for election campaigns. This book, however, focuses on an under-explored undercurrent in the daily news: the vast yet often inconspicuous media attention for public service providers. More specifically, it aims to describe and understand how public service providers interact with, and adapt to, their news media environments and traces and evaluates its consequences.

The book has been triggered by the simple observation that many scholars have noted that the provision of public services is increasingly affected by news media and that, to date, no systematic attempt has been made to analyze this phenomenon empirically. Most scholars noting the trend have done so with some concern or even alarm, as the news media are believed to have a "mutagenic effect" on policy processes (Mazzoleni & Schulz 1999: 249). Organizations dealing with the pressure from news media need to adapt their structures and processes in order to cope effectively. However, this process of adaptation may come at a high cost as the organization's identity may take a blow or even wither away. The citation from Timothy Cook's eminent *Governing with the News* (2005) that started this chapter already alluded to this risk. The quote aptly summarizes how the media's criteria for judging issues permeates policy processes and may accordingly affect and change important policy choices. The argument is that policy makers are judging issues more and more from the perspectives of relevance, importance and newsworthiness that are embodied in journalistic routines instead of using their own, independent, policy criteria (see Strömbäck 2011). This process, where the institutional logic of the media seeps into the operations of other organizations or social institutions, has in recent years been described as a process of *mediatization*. The organizations experiencing mediatization in this book are the many – public but also private – organizations delivering public services.

1.1 Public service providers

"[the change within the public services] is nothing less than a revolution in progress. Because it has been gradual, and has involved a high degree of co-operation by staff, it has not had the acknowledgement it deserves. Nor has the staff for their part in it. But it is a revolution, nonetheless, and its impact is dramatic." (John Major, quoted in Stewart & Walsh 1992).

The last decades witnessed many major reforms in the administration and governance of public services in most OECD-countries. Former UK Prime Minister John Major referred to those changes as a 'revolution-in-progress' and as something that would bring benefits to the organizations themselves and to citizens and customers alike. Although not many of the academic commentators are likely to share in his rosy appreciation, the trend to which he referred has been reinforced over time. The revolution refers to a wide set of changes in which established methods for delivering public services – organized in public organizations, directed by the central state and informed by legal and bureaucratic routines and procedures – were challenged around the globe. The challenge comes from the introduction of management techniques and organizational forms that were taken from the market. Many public services are now delivered by public agencies operating at arms' length of government as quasi-businesses; some of the services are even delivered by private organizations.

The term *new public management* is the overarching term with which a set of highly influential and related, yet not necessarily substantively coherent, public governance and organization ideas is usually described (Pollitt & Bouckaert 2004: 30; Hood 1991; Christensen & Laegreid 2011a; Peters 2001: 222). For the last two decades, new public management (NPM) has been the overriding intellectual trump card that shaped politician's decisions about the ways and the means with which to deliver public policies and services. In the shortest possible summary, NPM teaches that the public sector needs to learn from the private sector how to become more efficient, effective, flexible and responsive to the needs of citizens and customers (Noordegraaf 2000: 23). Public sector innovations in the Anglo Saxon countries have been dominant and have served as examples for developments in the rest of the western world, with the US and the UK in the lead and New Zealand and Australia as exciting and – to most continental Europeans – slightly exotic additional flavors.

As a general rule, NPM teaches that bureaucratic organizations are outdated because of their inability to deal with rising external demands in times of flexibility, turbulent innovations and emancipated and critical citizens. In this view, the old bureaucratic service providers closely resemble the poor old dinosaurs: they are just too big and too slow, their brain capacity is insufficient, so they are unable to adjust themselves timely and properly to ever changing external circumstances (Pollitt 2003: 32-3). In addition, as Niskanen and Downs taught in earlier decades, the bottom line business strategy of a bureaucracy is not to deliver services but is to ensure bureaucratic survival and budget maximation. NPM challenges the inbuilt incapacities of bureaucracies with a set of private sector measures, such as competition, performance targeting and -measurement and larger operational freedom for public managers within a tightened set of performance indicators and criteria (Hood 1991: 3; Pollitt 2003: 27). Public managers should accordingly have the freedom to actually *manage*, in order to deliver on clearly defined goals (Hood et al 1999: 197-8). Apart from the expected increases in efficiency, effectiveness and also accountability for results, the NPM-movement arose in response to the budgetary problems that many governments were – and currently are – facing. An integral feature and goal of many NPM-reforms has been to lower the levels of government spending on the organization and the delivery of public services (Pollitt & Bouckaert 2004: 16).

The effects of the string of NPM (and post-NPM, see Christensen & Laegreid 2011b) reforms on the provision of public services is that those services in most OECD-countries now are delivered by a myriad of different public, quasi-public and even private organizations. In countries such as the United Kingdom, the Scandinavian countries, New Zealand, and the Netherlands, many public agencies were hived off from the administrative centers of government departments and were reformed into quango's: quasi non-governmental organizations (see Verhoest et al 2010; James & Van Thiel 2011). The crucial point of *agentification* is that it allows the managers of public agencies more operational autonomy (see Pollitt 2003), something that has provoked widespread concerns regarding their accountability (see Schillemans 2011). Increasing their autonomy is supposed to be a necessary precondition that enables them to reap the benefits of effective organizational management and to transform rule-abiding bureaucracies into customer-oriented service providers. An even more rigorous method of ascertaining service provision by non-bureaucratic organizations is to delegate or outsource the provision of services to private, often non-profit or third sector, organizations. In many advanced countries, important public services such as housing, employment services, community services, education and health care, are, to some degree, delivered by non-profit organizations working on contracts or within public regulations. Champions of third sector service provision generally refer to the superior motivation of third sector organizations to provide services to people. As third sector organizations are driven by altruistic ideals and values, they are supposed – and often found – to be more innovative in their operations and to have greater commitment to their clients (see Kelly 2007).

Together, then, public services are generally, and to a rising degree, delivered by an organizational field that is of a substantial size and comes in a somewhat scattered form, featuring a large number of highly diverse organizations that span the boundaries of the public sector. Many large service providers also spend huge amounts of public money, as most things governments actually *do* are done through (semi-) public and (semi-) private agencies (Pollitt et al 2004).

The rising importance of the news media for politics and public policies has not gone unnoticed in the relatively "pastoral" (Pollitt et al 2004) world of public service providers. The claim is that every institution and organization in the field of public policy has had to adapt to the demands from the media environment. Again Cook (2005: 122) claims: "When one compares the 1950s and the 1990s (...) every branch of government is more preoccupied with and spends more resources on the news media today than it did forty years ago." His claim not only referred to the usual suspects in the White House and on Capitol Hill, but also to bureaucracies and the Supreme Court. A string of other scholars support his conclusion that the media have become an important external contingency for the civil service, public agencies and third sector organizations providing public services (see Gandy 1982; Weaver et al 2004: 268; Ward 2007; Young 2007: Xxxii; Mulgan 2002; Tiffen 1999: 196; Lyons 2001: 191; Dalton & Wilson

2009). Most authors, however, only *note* the importance of the media for public service providers or provide anecdotal evidence to the general trend. The impact of news media on public service providers, however, has received only sparse scholarly attention (Deacon & Monk 2001a; 2001b is the most notable exception. See also Besley & Burgess 2001; Carpenter 2002; Schillemans & Van Thiel 2009; Maggetti 2012).

There are various good reasons to investigate and assess the extent to which the news media affect the multifaceted organizations providing public services in western democracies. To begin with, the larger public agencies and third sector organizations devote substantial resources to monitoring, interacting and managing the news media (Ward 2007: 14; Mulgan 2002, 54; Savage & Tiffen 2007: 82). The introduction of private sector based approaches to service delivery naturally created space for more "ambitious" communication strategies, such as marketing (see Laing 2003) and branding (Eshuis & Klijn 2012). Separating the delivery of public services from national political centers also forced, or invited, managers of public service organizations to take a step forward into the spotlights of the media. Whereas most of these organizations themselves experience that journalists are often not too interested in their stories, they are collectively the subjects of a substantial volume of the daily news. As will be shown in chapter 4, the Dutch public and third sector providers of public services for instance feature in almost a third of all daily news stories in the quality press. The levels of reporting on service providers in Australia and the UK are even higher. This phenomenon is not specific for the Netherlands, as will be discussed in chapter 4, as the level of media coverage of public agencies is actually found to be even higher in the UK and in Australia.

The large, although not always very conspicuous and under-researched, news presence of public service providers speaks for the relevance of the issue in this book. Its relevance is further underscored by the host of concerned analyses of the supposedly undue influence of news media on politics and public policies.

1.2 Mediatization

"It is easy (as many do) to complain about the methods of new journalism. It hunts in packs, its eyes on bad news, egged on by the newsroom and bloggers saying that facts must never be allowed to get in the way of stories." (Keane 2009: 98)

Mediatization is the label carrying a general theory about how the media exert power over and in other social spheres. The literature on the mediatization of politics and public policies is connected to a larger body of work, where the rising prominence and intrusive character of the news media has provoked a string of concerned, or even alarmed, analyses, often epitomized in appealing book titles. Famous for instance are McChesney's *Rich Media, Poor Democracy* (1999), Entman's *Democracy without Citizens* (1989), Deacon and Golding's coinage of the *PR State* (see Ward 2007) and Meyer's *Media Democracy: How the Media Colonize Politics* (2002). Within this branch of the literature, the concern for spin doctoring and other forms of "political communication [that], say the critics, merely manufactures consent, rather than allow (…) discursive formulations of policy in the public interest" (Mayhew 1997: 5) has been enormous. In response, others questioned, downplayed or even contested the claim of undue media-influence (see Norris 1999; Kleinnijenhuis 2003).

Concerned commentators generally argue that the pressure from the news media may drive policy makers to focus their efforts and attention on the easy-to-communicate issues of the day to the detriment of the more complex and, arguably, more important question of the quality of service provision in the long run. The contention is that decision makers will be inclined towards the type of decisions that can be easily fit into the criteria for newsworthiness of journalists and, conversely, that they will be disinclined from taking the types of decisions that are hard to communicate in a ten second soundbite. This analysis is of acute importance for the organizations providing public services, as the quality of their services to a large degree rests on criteria that are not naturally newsworthy. The calamitous effects of mediatization on the quality of public services are thus, should this analysis at all be warranted, expected to manifest themselves here.

In the past years, many scholars have found the concept of *mediatization* useful in describing how the mass media are an agent of change for other institutions. The origins of the idea of mediatization can be traced back to Lippman's seminal work on *public opinion* (see Strömbäck 2011: 424). In more recent years, Kent Asp seems to be responsible for reintroducing the term, although he then preferred the slightly different spelling *medialization* (Asp 1990). The term was, not insignificantly, introduced with a quip, as Asp recalls:

"The term (…) [medialization, TS] is the product – I have to admit it – of a conscious effort on my part to coin a buzz word, a concept the media would pick up, a word that would filter into the stream of public discourse and gain currency among politicians and journalists alike. (…) To succeed in this, one has to invent something "catchy". Something that verges on the self-evident but still, at the same time, is vague enough so that each and everyone can read his own meaning into it." (Asp 1990: 47)

Asp went on to describe, with a reference to Adorno, that a good theory is like fly paper: everything sticks to it. These words, spoken at a conference in 1990, proved to be of a prophetic value. The concept 'mediatization' has since then made an impressive advance through all the sub fields of communication studies. It has been used by a large number of scholars in order to trace changes in practices, organizations and institutions in response to media-pressure. On the micro level, mediatization is used to analyze dyadic relationships between individuals – for instance: how many of the interactions with your partner are conducted through media? – and it has been used to study specific social interactions or practices, such as banking (Hjarvard 2008: 115), chess (ibid. 114) and many forms of play by children (Livingstone 2009: 7-9). On a meta level, mediatization has been used to analyze the development of society at large or of distinct social institutions, such as politics (Mazzoleni & Schulz 1999), religious life (Hoover 2009), performance (Auslander 1999), or consumption (Jansson 2002). There are even studies on the mediatization of the media themselves, for instance on the internetization of the (non-digital) media (Fortunati 2005) or the mediatization of television news (Strömbäck & Dimitrova 2011).

The proliferation of mediatization studies shows the effectiveness of Asp's 'conceptual communication strategy' with his fly paper theory. Broad, appealing and imprecise concepts can make quite an academic career, or so it seems. Scholars maximize the conceptual reach of the term and apply it to ever new objects of study, as can be seen from the merry hotchpotch of evolving mediatization studies. The proliferation of different and often unrelated mediatization studies, however, also has some important drawbacks. Livingstone (2009) pointed to this in her presidential address at the International Communication Association's annual conference, meaningfully entitled *the mediation of everything*. The title suggests that, when everything can be studied as an example of mediat(iza)ion, maybe it is nothing. More specifically, the term is sometimes used as a catch phrase rather than as a precise academic concept. As a result, the number of empirical studies of the mediatization of politics and public policies is still very limited. And in addition, even though there is a large volume of mediatization studies, we still know very little about the adaptation processes supposedly engendered by media-pressure on politics and policies.

This book is intellectually related to a number of recent scholarly projects (Kepplinger 2002; Schulz 2004; Krotz 2007; Strömbäck 2008; 2011; Hjarvard 2008), where authors seek to develop and test stricter and more precise understandings of mediatization, in order to be able to improve our empirical insights in the process. The aim is, metaphorically speaking, to transform the original fly-paper-concept into a filtering concept that sifts and selects in order to thicken our insights and to improve the quality of the residue of knowledge.

1.3 The plan of the book

This books aims to shed light on the impact of the news media on public and third sector organizations providing public services. It basically seeks to describe and understand the ways in which the news media have become an influential, external force that shapes, and possibly changes, public and third sector organizations providing public services. The book adopts a programmatically *empirical* (and not normative or theoretical) approach to the highly *normative* issue of media influence on public service providers. It provides a first systematic analysis of the mediatization of public service providers on the basis of extensive research. It is based on a dual comparative research design, comparing organizations in two countries of rather different size but with fairly similar numbers of inhabitants – i.e. Australia and the Netherlands – and compares public with third sector organizations providing public services. The comparisons provide insights into the different ways in which media environments affect different types of organizations providing different types of services. The book focuses on the generic characteristics and findings that came forward in our research, leaving the strict comparison between the two principal countries for different occasions (see Schillemans 2010). By focusing on the mediatization of public services, the book connects two generally unrelated strands of social science research: the political communication research on mediatization with public administration research on public agencies and public service delivery.

The contention that underlies the book is that it is necessary for providers of public services to cope strategically with their media environments, as the media can be critical assets in relation to important resources such as funding, reputations, and legitimacy; resources also that can be reinvested to realize one's mission. However, in order to be able to interact successfully with the news media, organizations need to go through some organizational changes that may be highly consequential for the ways they understand and execute their tasks and ultimately for their mission and identity. In an optimistic scenario, organizations may learn how to serve their mission in an environment of media pressure. In a pessimistic scenario, however, organizations will gradually change and lose sight of their true mission and become preoccupied with 'keeping up appearances'. This research project initially aims to map the impact of news media and the different approaches to media from different organizations. In doing so, it will sketch a vivid picture of the complex and often covert interactions between media and public service providers.

The book's structure is as follows. The first two *theoretical* chapters will discuss and relate the two central concepts of public service provision (chapter 2) and mediatization (chapter 3). The next four *empirical* chapters will systematically describe how news media exert pressure on public service providers (chapter 4) and how these organizations in turn use media as sources of information (mediatization of inputs, chapter 5), how they adapt their internal structures and processes (mediatization of throughputs, chapter 6) and how media work is integrated into their core functions and service provision (mediatization of outputs, chapter 7). The book concludes with two *evaluative* chapters. The first analyses how public service providers use, for better or for worse, *and* are hindered by the special traits of media logic (chapter 8). The ninth and final chapter, then, condenses the main findings in the book and tentatively explores some the implications and ways forward. Before take-off, however, some comments need to be made about the research project and the data on which this book is based.

1.4 Researching mediatization

Mapping the mediatization of public services is a journey across a relatively barren territory as there is little existing empirical research on mediatization, let alone research with a focus on the mediatization of public organizations, to build on. The research project was driven by a large number of tentative expectations across a broad range of issues and was not guided by a specific and directing theoretical model or by specific hypotheses. In consequence, the general research strategy has been to use a variety of research methods in order to be able to arrive at a large set of empirical outcomes.

The generic tale about the mediatization of public service providers in this book is based on a comparative research project focusing on Australian and Dutch service providers. A comparison between the Netherlands and Australia reads as a *most different case* design (see Meckstroth 1975). As will be explained in the next chapter, Australia and the Netherlands represent two extremes within the spectrum of western countries. The countries differ substantially, both in terms of governance structures as in terms of media systems. A most different case design is then helpful as a means to come to grips with important differences and contrasts, as well as overarching similarities, between countries and between organizations. It allows us to sketch a comprehensive view of the main features and general structure of the issue. In addition, it is relevant to note that there are some excellent comparative studies on Australian and Dutch public policies (Considine & Lewis 2003a and 2003b; Bevir, Rhodes & Weller 2003; Smullen 2007).

The comparative approach is furthermore also very helpful as mediatization is a process that develops *over time*. Investigating organizational and policy processes over time is however a difficult task, especially when we are interested in internal routines and processes that are not directly tangible and cannot be reliably deducted from organizational charts, financial indicators or available statistics. A comparative approach between countries and between different organizations is then a helpful and insightful second best option to the problematically time-consuming number one option of historical reconstruction.

Finally, the comparative approach is also helpful as mediatization is not a digital concept (organizations either are or are not mediatized) but rather is an analogous concept, that allows for gradual levels of mediatization. The comparative approach will naturally produce a yardstick by which forms of mediatization can be compared. Should we just focus on one case, it would be very hard the make sense of the outcomes.

The explorative research design has cast a relatively wide net. The guiding idea is *triangulation*: using a combination of research methods in a fact-finding mission on the adaptation of service providers to their media environments. The research methods will be described in short below. The appendix provides a full description of the different elements of the research project.

Content analysis of media coverage

The media coverage of Australian and Dutch service providers has been researched in three data sets. The aim was first to establish the level of media reporting on public service providers and to assess the levels and the content of the media pressure on these organizations. Aim of this part of the research was to establish whether public service providers actually experience a considerable level of media pressure and to analyze trends and characteristics in reporting.

The **first data set** looked at long term trends in reporting on public service providers in Australia, the Netherlands and the UK. This data set accumulates all the stories on a list of public service providers and search words in a limited number of quality newspapers for each country over the 13-year period 1999-2011. The comparison with the UK was used as a benchmark and chosen because of the relevance of prior work in the UK by Deacon and Monk (2001a, b). Analysis of a limited number of quality newspapers is common in communications research, as earlier investigations exposed the large overlap in media agendas between different newspapers (McCombs 2004; Arnold 2004). The general pattern in a limited number of newspapers may thus be assumed to be representative for the general trend. The media stories were retrieved via search engine Factiva (for the UK and Australia) and through LexisNexis (for the Netherlands).

The **second data set** looked at the same list of organizations but widened its focus to all media stories, whilst simultaneously narrowing its focus to (mostly) 2008. The second data set had a threefold aim. The shorter timeframe allowed us to add more depth to the analysis of the stories. It for instance enabled us to assess the levels of personalization of Chief Executive Officers (CEOs) of service providers in news stories. The shorter timeframe also allowed us to look closer at the intensity of news waves. Organizations are never haunted by a single news story but it is rather the suddenness and the overwhelming and repetitive nature of news coverage across all media outlets that astounds and sometimes scares the subjects of sudden coverage. It is the *pack journalism* quality of the news that is important and this aspect could be tapped in the second data set. The shorter time frame finally allowed us to make a comparison of the levels of news coverage between service providers and a set of national politicians.

The **third data set** focused on only one newspaper in each country (Sydney Morning Herald and the Volkskrant) and aimed to analyze all the stories on public service providers in all domestic news stories. This required intensive coding of all organizations mentioned in all stories with the help of two research assistants and the program atlas.ti. In total 695 stories were analyzed and coded. With this intensive scope of analysis, an assessment could be made of the relative number of stories on public service providers in the national news. And the short time frame furthermore allowed us to analyze the news frames in which public service providers are described. It for instance allowed us to analyze the relative number of negative news items on organizations and to relate differences in types of coverage to different types of organizations.

Content analysis of organizational websites

The websites of a selection of 56 large Australian and Dutch public service providers have been analyzed and coded in order to assess the varying degrees to which these websites cater for the news media. The idea was basically to assess to what degree the organizational websites assisted journalists in crafting their stories. In this content analysis, questions such as the following were posed: How easy is it to find the name and number of press officers, the availability of background facts and figures, printable photos of CEOs or rss-subscriptions, etc.

Focus groups

The mediatization of public organizations was furthermore assessed in a series of focus groups. The focus groups consisted of 4 to 9 representatives from coherent sets of organizations: public service providers within or outside of government departments, third sector organizations providing public services, and regulatory agencies. The focus groups had a fixed format, where participants were first asked to formulate their first associations on the role of the media, then they filled out a small questionnaire and then a group discussion evolved that was guided by four general questions. The general questions concerned the use of media as sources of information (media as inputs, see ch. 5), the quality of journalistic reporting, the news as a threat to organizations and how they cope with that threat (ch. 6) and the media as a strategic asset that can be exploited by organizations (ch. 7). The total number of respondents in the focus groups was 42.

Small scale survey

As noted above, all participants in the focus groups filled in a questionnaire with 22 items. The questionnaires were also returned by a number of contacted respondents from organizations who were unable to participate on the given day. The total number of respondents was 50. The idea of the survey was first of all to countervail some of the effects of the group processes in the focus groups. The survey covered the same questions as the discussions in the focus group. It also served to give quantitative outcomes on a four-point scale in contrast to the qualitative outcomes of discussions. It also served as a check: the survey sometimes revealed suppressed variance among participants.

Elite interviews

Finally, elite interviews were held with executives or strategic officers from public service providers on the mediatization of their organizations and the strategies they use. The focus on just one respondent and organization allowed for more depth of analysis than is possible in focus groups with a variety of participants, and it allowed the respondents to speak more freely. There were 4 'background' interviews in Australia, and 18 elite interviews in both Australia and in the Netherlands. The total number of respondents, thus, was 40.

All respondents have participated in this research project on the basis of full anonymity. There is no list with names or organizations available and there is also no correlation between the organizations that were analyzed in the content analyses and the participants in focus groups and elite interviews. The empirical chapters are all to a large degree based on quotes from the interviews and focus groups. All quotes have been anonymized and information that relates to specific issues, organizations, functions, times or persons, has been cut from the quotes.

Table 1 below provides an overview of the different research methods and shows how they helped to shape the different chapters in the book.

Table 1: Overview research questions & research methods

	Data set 1	Data set 2	Data set 3	Website analysis	Focus groups	Survey	Elite interviews
Ch. 4 Media pressure	×	×	×		×	×	×
Ch. 5 Mediatization of inputs					×	×	×
Ch. 6 Mediatization of throughputs					×	×	×
Ch. 7 Mediatization of outputs			×	×	×	×	×
Ch. 8 Media logic					×	×	×

2. Public services

"... The clear set of governmental organizations and public service providers of the past has been supplanted by a host of independent agencies, hybrid public-private partnerships, voluntary agreements, ethical codes and gentlemen's agreements (...) The result is that central government has been transformed into a multi-headed animal (...) Yesterday's governmental organization may well have turned into a private company by today or – even worse – into an entity somehow dangling in the middle." (Vuijsje 2005: 29).

The organization and management of public services has changed dramatically over the past decades. Where the former British Prime Minister Major, as discussed in the previous chapter, spoke warmly of those changes and compared their combined impact to a silent revolution, the Dutch sociologist and publicist Vuijsje cast them in a rather dim light. He even went on to suggest that contemporary public organizations are inclined to fission and mutation. Whatever the normative appreciation of those changes is, however, irrespective of the question whether we have been witnessing a revolution or a process of uncontrollable mutation, the underlying developments are beyond dispute. The waves of recent government reforms have created ever more complex systems of public service provision in most advanced democracies, where the boundaries between state, market and civil society have become increasingly blurred.

Consider the employment services in the Netherlands. Employment services first became a governmental task in 1930 and remained, although with some major reshufflings and rearrangements in structures, organization and management, a system that was regulated and operated on an exclusively public basis until 1991 (Van der Meer & Visser 2004; Bekke & Van Gestel 2004). Since then, four successive major reforms (1991, 1996, 2002, and 2009) followed in which the exercise of authority and the division of operational responsibilities were rearranged. At first, the public monopoly on employment services was broken and representatives from employers and trade unions were included in decision making and service delivery. This means that *third sector organizations* were now granted, although only for a couple of years, an important role in the delivery of public services. The tripartite experiment was, however, abandoned after just a few years (1996), following a major policy crisis. The sector was now prepared for a large scale *privatization* of services. For a few years, *market organizations* were considered to be the most efficient operators of the system. The existing organizations started their preparations for privatization in what was surely pleasurable anticipation. Political fortunes, however, made a new turn and the services were not privatized in 2002, but to a large degree concentrated in two independent public agencies, while some minor tasks were outsourced to the for-profit sector and some other tasks were decentralized to local authorities. In the years since then, a number of additional tasks were delegated to local authorities, while the two newly instituted independent public agencies were merged in 2009.

In short, the provision of employment services bounced back and forth between central and local governments, between public and private organizations and between the interests of employers and unions (Van der Meer & Visser 2004: 184). Interestingly, the actual organizations – the offices, the people, and the files – were often continued. Changes mainly affected the distribution of tasks and revenues in the network of organizations and their administrative-legal status. Vuijsje's concern about public organizations muting into ever new species, forms and constellations is at least to some degree fuelled by this sequence of organizational changes.

Public sector reform and changing boundaries between the private and the public sector are by no means restricted to just the issue of employment services in just the Netherlands. The international waves of public management and public services reform have been documented in a number of excellent studies (Pollitt & Bouckaert 2004; Christensen & Laegreid 2011a; Lecy & Van Slyke 2012; Pollitt 2012) and it is beyond the scope of this book to trace the many changes in public service provision over the last decade. This chapter will rather focus on three more constricted issues which are of direct relevance to the mediatization of organizations. At first, the rather general concept of 'public service providers' will be unpacked, and a number of typologies will be introduced with which the sometimes bewildering variety of organizational types can be understood. Secondly, some important characteristics of the reforms in public service provision in Australia and the Netherlands need to be discussed as this provides necessary context for the evolving narrative on the mediatization of service providers based on our research in these countries. Thirdly, some key tensions in the provision of public services will be addressed as a background to the tale of organizational mediatization.

2.1 A diversity of public service providers

The growing organizational complexity in contemporary public service provision has been accompanied by a choir of initially concerned academic commentators.

A canonic commentary was Rhodes' (1994) on the *hollowing out of the state,* which he saw as the sum total of evolving trends in service provision, such as delegation to independent agencies, privatization to non-public organizations and alternative service delivery systems. The nature of traditional British democratic rule, and by extension that of other western democracies, was severely undermined by the many changes that saw executive power move away from the reigns of central administrations. The cluster of evolving organizations has been understood as *non-majoritarian institutions* (Thatcher & Stone Sweet 2002) or as *the Unelected* (Vibert 2007). Both descriptions focus on the dissociation of executive powers from the electoral process. Keane even went one step further and fitted those changes in a general description of *post-representative democracy* (Keane 2009). The organizations in this sub field of public service provision now span the boundaries between the public and the private. Furthermore, it is now common to understand that advanced democracies feature increasingly blurred systems of partially public and partially private service provision (Rainey 2009: 62) and that we face an increasingly confusing mix of elements from state, market and civil society in the "management of public affairs" (Thynne 2003: 317; see Wettenhall 2003). The diversity of public service providers can be ordered along a number of dimensions: organizational types, organizational tasks and organizational characteristics.

Organizational types

Real organizational forms generally precede academic organizational classifications and those classifications, in turn, are generally based on unique national experiences. As a result, the variety of existing public services eschews easy attempts at categorization. Over the last years, however, numerous scholars have come up with organizational classifications for public and private organizations, which are seldom exhaustive but nevertheless provide a suitable basis for the analysis of public agencies and third sector service providers. There are different typologies for public and for third sector organizations. Those typologies depart from clearly diverging starting points but end up displaying some overlapping, even interchangeable, types.

James & Van Thiel (2011: 210; see also Thynne 2003) introduced a six-part typology for *public* organizations, which works well for the analysis of public service providers. The point of departure of their model is the more or less implicit assumption that the default option for public service delivery is *national* service delivery. This entails that the service is delivered by a public bureaucracy under full ministerial responsibility of a minister who is accountable to Parliament and, by implication, to the general public. This is their first category of public sector organizations, where a unit or directory of a national or federal government is responsible for a given task. The other five types of organizations are all deviances from this default option, where the national minister's formal control on the execution of a policy is increasingly compromised.

The second type of organizations is formed by *semi-autonomous public agencies*. These agencies exist in many democracies, where they are generally situated within government departments but are exempted from customary hierarchical control on specified dimensions of their operations, such as staffing, budgeting or communications. The third set of organizations consists of *fully independent public agencies*. They are legally independent, are generally enacted in public law and their operations are based on statutes. The public managers in these agencies enjoy, at least theoretically if not always in practice, considerable levels of managerial autonomy (Pollitt 2003). The fourth cluster of public agencies is formed, somewhat surprisingly perhaps, by *private organizations established by or on behalf of the government*, such as foundations, corporations, and some enterprises. The key feature of this type of organization is that of continuous public ownership of essentially private entities. The establishment of the organization allows for governmental control, be it through direct intervention, appointments or the prerogative to terminate the organization. For the companies in this category, the state is the only, or at least the majority, owner of stocks. The fifth (actually, the sixth in the original ordering of James and Van Thiel 2011) set of organizations is even one step further removed from the state and consists of fully autonomous private organizations, where the government owes no or just a minority of the stock. These organizations may still operate as public service providers, not in terms of ownership or through their enactment, however, but through either public regulation or public funding. It is a bit of a paradox, perhaps, now to note that this attempt at categorizing different types of *public* organizations brings us to a set of almost entirely *private* organizations. The last set of organizations in James & Van Thiel's (2011) typology of public sector organizations are regional or local public bodies and authorities. These organizations are not distinguished from the default option 'national bureaucracy' by their increased private nature, but by the devolution of executive power to lower levels of governance. This organizational type could actually be, and in effect is, combined with the other organizational types, as there are also local public agencies and locally established public enterprises.

As for public agencies, there are numerous existing typologies of *third sector organizations*. These typologies generally seek to establish the unique and differentiating characteristics of a field of organizations that stands out from both state and market. Surprisingly, perhaps, attempts at categorization of these essentially non-state entities always bring the state back in as an important defining characteristic.

The text book example of categorization in this field comes from Salamon and Anheier (1992). Their definition of the third sector turned out to be highly useful and has formed the basis of a blossoming field of comparative studies of the third sector. The central problem of all definitions of the third sector, or in definitions of related concepts such as civil society, is that their principal defining characteristic is of a negative nature. The third sector is initially defined by what it is *not* – it is neither state nor market; neither first nor second sector – but it is not directly evident which positive features are inherent in the concept. Legally trained scholars have sought to base the distinctiveness of the third sector in legal definitions; economists have preferred financial definitions, while social scientists tended to rely on functional definitions that focus on what the organizations *do*. These definitions come a long way, but nevertheless fail to distinguish third sector organizations definitively from the other two sectors. To this end, Salamon and Anheier turned to a more complex *structural / operational* definition. This approach encapsulates elements from the other three approaches and combines them into a definition that sports five key characteristics of third sector organizations.

To begin with, third sector organizations are *formal organizations* which are, at least to some extent, institutionalized. This first defining characteristic ensures that third sector organizations can be distinguished from the wealth of existing voluntary networks, activities and other forms of everyday societal, collective action. The second trait of third sector organizations is that they are *private* organizations which are institutionally and legally distinctive from the state. On the traditional public – private dichotomy, they find themselves at the same end of the spectrum as private businesses. Third sector organizations however, and that is the third element in this general definition, stand out from businesses by *non-profit distributing*. This means that the organizations serve non-profit goals, and that they use their incomes, profit and revenues in order to maintain and, where possible, expand operations. Third sector organizations are furthermore in meaningful ways self-organizing and self-governing. Some third sector organizations may have been instituted by or on behalf of either the state or private enterprises; being able to govern and organize themselves turns those organizations into integral parts of the third sector. The fifth and final defining characteristic is that third sector organizations rely in either management or operations on voluntary participation.

This last element in the Salamon and Anheier typology is somewhat puzzling. Where the first and fourth criteria clearly serve to establish that the organization actually is an *organization*, and the second and third criteria serve to exclude public organizations and private businesses, the functionality of this last criterion is less apparent. Voluntary participation is probably an empirically and descriptively important element of third sector organizations; it is not obvious why this necessarily and prescriptively needs to be a defining trait of organizations occupying the sphere between private households, the market and the state.

Whatever the status of this element of voluntarism, however, for our purposes the relationship to the state is the most important element in the typology. As defined, third sector organizations need independence from the state, or so the conventional tale goes. This does not imply, however, that the third sector is fully unrelated to the state. That would be truly inconceivable as both spheres are active in the provision of services to people. Coston (1998) has convincingly described how the relationships between third sector organizations and the state can be ordered on a scale that starts with outright mutual hostility and ends with active collaboration in a context of institutional plurality. Coston described some potential relationships on this continuum.

Her point can be clarified by the example of a third sector organization offering educational services. At the one extreme of the scale, the state could try to ban or prosecute the organization for offering education ("repression"), see the service as an unhelpful alternative for the preferential public schools ("rivalry") or consider the service as a neutral alternative and leave it to citizens to decide for themselves ("competition"). In all three cases, the public service provided by the third sector organization is a competitor to the available public service, which is treated with a decreasing level of hostility. In the next three potential relationships, the third sector develops into the actual provider of the public service, on an ever more permanent basis. It could be that the organization provides education on a temporary basis and within stipulated parameters ("contracting"). It could also be that there is a division of labor between state and third sector, where government defines and regulates public services which, in turn, are organized and delivered by third sector organizations ("third-party government"). Or it could be that the relationship evolves into a full "cooperation", characterized by a free flow of information and mutual respect and acceptance. Where this cooperation brings forward advantages from both state and third sector, Coston dubs this as "complementarity" and where the third sector organizations are handed decision making power, she understands the relationship as "collaboration".

More or less implicit in Coston's typology of the relationships between the state and third sector organizations is that the sharp division between the two gradually develops into a more blurred relationship. At this extreme of her continuum of relationships, tasks and decision making have become overlapping and the relationships are fixed on a long-term basis. Here, third sector organizations evolve into quasi-governmental organizations ("quago's"), which should ring a bell, as the prior typology of public agencies ended with quasi nongovernmental organizations ("quango's"). Both typologies, thus, land on the same ground: a mixed zone where organizations are hybrids or half-bloods; simultaneously partially embedded in the third sector and partially connected to and directed by the state.

Typologies of tasks

The organizations on the gliding scale from public to third sector deliver a large volume of very different types of services. Some of those services require expert judgment where others depend on bureaucratic attention to detail and procedure; some are delivered by monopolists where others flourish in complex markets, and some services are provided by enormous *machine bureaucracies* where others are operated by just a handful of professionals and volunteers. Within this broad pallet of different flavors, a number of distinctions are important.

A first important distinction relates to the *policy area* where services are delivered. In a large scale international, comparative study, Verhoest et al (2010) categorized the tasks of public organizations in three broad categories: welfare and social policy; economic policy and a broad 'others' category. The last category obviously includes the largest variety of tasks but the first two include the largest number of organizations.

A further useful distinction was made by Van Thiel (2006) in her typology of public tasks. She discriminated between six types of public tasks: maintenance (of buildings, data bases, etc.); payment or collection of benefits; inspection and regulation (& enforcement); training, research and communication; registration and licensing; and tribunals. This typology was derived from an analysis of Dutch independent public agencies and left an important area of public service delivery aside: professional public services, such as medical care and social housing. These seven categories grossly cover the variety of public services offered in democracies.

Within this set of public services, two more distinctions are necessary (Laing 2003). The first relates to the relationships to the beneficiaries of the services. Some services are delivered with a high degree of personal contact with the public where others are more anonymous and delivered with a low degree of contact with the public. This distinction can be combined with the degree to which the customer pays for a service. Furthermore, public services strike a balance between social and private benefits and operate on the basis of (a combination of) either professional or consumer judgment. Where social benefits, collective finance and professional judgment prevail, it is most likely that the service will be delivered by a public agency. And where private benefits, individualized pay and consumer judgment prevails, it is hard to argue for public service provision.

Organizational characteristics

The public-private dichotomy is not only helpful to distinguish between organizational types; it is also an important distinction shaping the *internal* form of service providers. Many organizations will inhibit public elements alongside private elements. The public character of the organization can be located in one or more of three loci. Organizations may be considered partially public when they operate on the basis of i) public law, are ii) financed by public funding or serve iii) public values. Public values stand in contrast to economic values; public values relate in Moore's important definition (see Rainey 2009: 68-70) to organizational outputs that are rooted in the desires and perceptions of individuals. As public values are derived from the values that people adhere to, and as people's opinions and perceptions are prone to change, it is impossible to provide a finite list of all public values. The importance of the concept is rather that it serves as a basis with which to legitimate why public resources are set of to provide given services to people.

Following Thynne (2003) it may be stated that public organizations can be distinguished along five organizational criteria, where different combinations of public and private traits can be found. To begin with, all organizations are established by some *legal instrument,* be it of private or of public law. Furthermore, patterns of *ownership* can fluctuate. Some public service organizations are owned and administered by public actors, where some other organizations are fully in the hands of private entities. A third important descriptive element of organizations is the *financing arrangement.* Here, various combinations of public and private funding generally exist, which makes it very hard to distinguish public from private organizations on this characteristic. Thynne (2003: 327) wrote:

> "The essence of these arrangements is that state and non-state organizations often cannot be differentiated on the basis of finance alone. (…) This can mean that their control and accountability requirements are similar as they look inward to the state when state finance is involved and outward to the market and civil society when using finance from members, customers, clients, and so on".

Staffing arrangements and *outsourcing* initiatives are two more elements of organizations which can be either public or private. The questions are, is the staff considered to be state employees and is the public organization performing all of the work itself or have elements of production been outsourced to other private organizations.

These five elements can be combined in order to create different types of (quasi) public and (quasi) private organizations. On the one hand you can find legally public organizations working on private funding with non-state employees; on the other hand there are formally private organizations spending public money in order to serve public values.

2.2 Public service provision in Australia and the Netherlands

This book covers the generic topic of the mediatization of public service providers on the basis of comparative research in Australia and the Netherlands. We will now shortly set the scene of our inquiry and discuss some important features of public service provision in the two countries. Australia and the Netherlands seem an odd pair, perhaps, at first glance. There is a large geographical divide between Australia and the Netherlands. The countries are located at opposite sides of the globe, occupy hugely different territories but inhabit remarkably similar, 16 versus 22 million, numbers of inhabitants. Both countries have also in some ways been at the forefront of the waves of new public management reforms that swept through the developed world since the 1990s (Christensen & Laegreid 2011a; Smullen 2007).

Dutch public services at a glance

In the Netherlands, there have been large government reforms that were more or less explicitly inspired by new public management thinking, although it is sometimes hard to tell rhetoric from real organizational changes. A substantial field of reform has been the delivery of public services. In its dependence on micro economic theory, this innovation has been a clear break with established tradition in the Netherlands. To the effect that the separation of policy delivery from policy formulation adds to the fragmentation of the political system as a whole, the separation of public agencies from the center was actually a reinforcement of the existing governance tradition.

In fields such as education, health care, social housing and community services, Dutch governments have always strongly relied on third sector organizations for delivering services, within a framework of public regulation and on the basis of public expenditures (WRR 2004; Brandsen et al 2010). On the national level, there is a large and complex network of more or less autonomous government agencies delivering most national services. The late nineteen eighties and early nineteen nineties witnessed the programmatic creation of independent agencies at arm's length of central government. The development was in line with developments across the world (Politt et al 2004; Verhoest et al 2010).

From the mid nineteen nineties onwards, most service providers on the central governmental level were given some operational autonomy from policy making government departments. In the past years, however, this trend has been reversed and the level of central control on independent agencies has increased.

Public services are now provided by a large number of organizations that are not fully and directly accountable to ministers. They spend a little more than 100 billion euro's annually (Vermeer et al 2004: 17) and employ more people than central government (Van Thiel 2000: 39). There are hundreds of quangos in the Netherlands, some 45 often large and partially autonomous agencies within government departments, and there are many more service providers in the health care, welfare, social housing and education services.

Australian public services at a glance

The strong Australian federal government has also been an international forerunner and role model in the public sector reforms on an NPM basis. Federal reforms have often served as a 'laboratory' of reforms that were later redeveloped and refined in the various Australian states (Pollitt & Bouckaert 2004: 210-1). Typical NPM-ideas about total quality management, benchmarking and performance targeting found fertile soil in Australian governance. Nevertheless, a strong sense of a distinctive public service remained (Rhodes et al 2008). The reforms have overall been described as the introduction of a 'Market bureaucracy' (Considine 1996): the public sector now combines elements from markets and business practices with reinforced forms of administrative control and some centralization.

Australian public services are delivered by a broad variety of public agencies and third sector organizations, just as in the Netherlands, although there are some important differences in form. Many of the social services that in the Netherlands are delivered by third sector organizations are in Australia delivered through the public agencies of the different states: social housing, education, health care and some community services. On the national level, there is a variety of public agencies that are generally directly answerable to the minister. A number of often complex tasks or regulatory services are delivered by a host of statutory authorities (Wettenhall 2003; Aulich et al 2010). In the course of the nineteen nineties there have been some experiments with new types of more independent agencies, such as executive agencies or prescribed agencies (Smullen 2007). The level of autonomy of these agencies however decreased over the last years as the Australian political center has 'reasserted its control' (Halligan 2006). There has been some notable centralization in the agency domain under the Howard governments, mainly for reasons of accountability (Macintosh 2007: 152).

In some areas, notably employment and community services, there has however and simultaneously been a large shift away from the center by forms of competitive tendering of services to many third sector organizations, often with a religious foundation (McDonald & Marston 2002; Schwartz 1994; Saunders & Stewart-Weeks 2009; Lyons 2001). The underlying idea is to contract out services to the best bid in terms of quality and costs, where private organizations can compete for contracts with (former) government agencies. Some third sector organizations have been very active and have become renown in these new 'markets' of publicly funded social services, such as the Smith Family, Mission Australia and the KU Children Services (Lyons 2001). The development has been described as a corporatist model of service delivery, where government finances third sector organizations that support households (Saunders 2009: 9). The overall share of government funding in the total revenue of the third sector is considerable. Grossly a third of the total revenue of the approximately 700.000 Australian third sector organizations comes from government grants and contracts (Lyons 2009). In fields such as community services, health, education, social housing and employment, government funding accounts for almost half of the total incomes (Lyons 2001). Overall, Australian third sector organizations thus play an important role in the delivery of public services and they constitute a large – although smaller than in the Netherlands – part of the fragmented landscape of public service provision.

The Dutch and Australian landscapes of public service provision thus display some important commonalities and these are not atypical throughout the western administrative world. The Netherlands on the one hand has a long tradition of semi-corporatist governance where public services have always to a large extent been provided by third sector organizations (Brandsen et al 2010). Australia on the other hand has a similar yet smaller tradition (Lyons 2001), which has been reinvigorated in the past years when numerous public services were contracted out to third sector organizations. Simultaneously, many public services are in both countries delivered by statutory bodies, independent commissions and other – more or less – independent public agencies.

2.3 Tensions in public service provision

Public service providers operate on the nexus between state power, markets, and society. Public service providers are, in various ways and to varying degrees, linked to the political system but they nevertheless should and do have some real organizational autonomy. Service providers are also linked to the persons, groups or territories benefiting from their services, although the levels of contact and partisanship vary. And many service providers operate in de facto markets where private service providers may challenge their position and where they may have to adhere to market laws and regulations. Public service providers should be responsive to their political environment, customer friendly *and* competitive in and compliant with the market. Public service providers, in short, have 'multiple legitimate masters' (Posner 2002) which strongly affects their strategic behavior and invokes a number of tensions.

Political tensions

The political system is of obvious importance to public service providers as the public character of services ultimately rests on political decision making. It is essentially a matter of jurisdiction: to what extent are the service providers themselves able to make and adjust strategic issues and in what ways is their behavior controlled by the government, the administration, and Parliament. Some political systems provide a relatively high degree of autonomy to service providers where others are found to be more strictly centrally controlled. These tensions will be explored below, where we focus our discussion on the differences between Australia and the Netherlands, as they are useful antipodes in this respect.

The Dutch political system is an example where service providers have traditionally been granted important degrees of autonomy. The Dutch political system was famously described by Lijphart as a form of consociational democracy. Consociationalism refers to the fragmented but surprisingly stable form of democracy that was traditionally found in countries such as the Netherlands, Belgium and Austria (Lijphart 1969: 211). It is a *fragmented* system as numerous societal sub groups are represented in Parliament by a large number of political parties. The proportional system in those countries generally assures the election of a large number of parties to Parliament. The general election of 2010 for instance brought ten parties to the Dutch Parliament, where the largest party only had around a fifth of the vote (and the seats) and the fifth party still obtained a tenth of the vote. Coalition governments with two or three parties are generally necessary in this context. The political institutions of consociationalism compel party elites to cooperate across party boundaries. Those elites have to be more sensitive and respectful towards the others than is common in dualistic political systems as they know that they may be forced to cooperate in a coalition government in the near future. This anticipation-of-cooperation basically lowers the levels of political antagonism in Parliament. The cooperation between elites ensures the stability of the democratic system but also leads to a spread of responsibilities and institutions, as the different parties in a coalition government carve up the 'benefits' of the office and divide the spoils among a large number of beneficiaries. The Netherlands have a recognized reputation of dispersed governance, where numerous political and societal actors are involved in decision making processes and service provision.

The Australian political system, in contrast, is much more centralized as is common in Westminster democracies (Roberts 2005: 20; Smullen 2007: 270). The 'first around the post' electoral system normally – although not in the 2010 national elections – provides either Labor or the coalition with an absolute majority and majoritarian rule is thus normal. The political concentration of power spills over into the public service, where the level of centralization is also much higher as the prime minister's relative powers are much stronger than those of her counterpart in the Netherlands, who is generally considered as nothing but the primus inter pares of a group of equally weighted ministers. The virtual two-party system of Australia lowers the necessity for cooperation between the political antagonists and this – perhaps together with some cultural features – explains the strongly antagonistic features of Australian political life, particularly when compared to the political tradition in the Netherlands. Smullen for instance described Australian Parliament as: "*An unruly bear pit in which politics is a ruthless adversarial contest between disciplined parties*" (Smullen 2007: 268). The de facto quasi two-party political system adds potential politicization of services to the expected levels of centralization, which has raised some concern (Barns 2005; Hamilton & Maddison 2007).

Market tensions

Where public services are delivered by organizations that operate in close proximity to markets, a number of tensions arise. First of all, the provision of a service may be seen to disrupt the market and drive out private competition. The proliferation of public service providers in the NPM-era that cross the traditional boundaries of the state has aggravated this in itself ageless issue. In response to this tension, governments around the globe have erected and strengthened their independent competition authorities and have redrafted and revised competition laws and market regulations.

A second tension follows from the dependence on finances in markets. Some public and third sector service providers operate on market revenues. This can be beneficial, as some of the services lend themselves well to direct payments by clients and as the pricing mechanism may allow the organization to tailor-make their services to the demands of their clients. The flip side of the coin is, of course, that the dependency on market revenues may also impede the organization's maneuverability. It may hamper organizations that need to change their course of action. And conversely, the necessity to attract revenues may force service providers to pursue courses of action that stand at odds with their true mission (*mission creep*).

A third important tension relates to the confusing accountability demands with which public service providers are faced when they operate in markets. Klingner et al (2002) described a case of policy reform where foster care was contracted out to private suppliers. This reform was infused with different expectations, resulting in multiple, diverse, changing and conflicting pressures on the participants. The conflicting expectations, amongst others, followed from the fact that in this case, a new combination of politics with administration and market elements was sought. Politics, administrations, and markets relate to separate ways of decision-making that produce different expectations of accountability which are often at odds with each other.

Societal tensions

Many public service providers, particularly those whose work involves frequent contacts with their clients, operate in social networks. This proximity to their clients is bound to foster warm bonds of loyalty between the recipients and the providers of the service. This is even truer for third sector organizations providing public services as they are generally based on societal foundations. The use of third sector organizations has, as was explained above, been understood as a corporatist model of service delivery (Saunders 2009). This is believed by many to improve the quality of the services and has been the basis for contracting third sector organizations to provide public services (Kelly 2007; Saunders 2009). In some areas, such as specifically community services and employment, many policy makers suspect that third sector organizations will outperform traditional bureaucratic service providers, as their internal motivation for the job and their specialized knowledge of issues, clients and local circumstances is higher. Also, the levels of red tape and bureaucratic stasis are believed to be lower and the more radical separation of roles in the purchaser-provider model of delivery aims to provide a push for efficiency. As third sector organizations are deliberately established to serve specific social causes, and as government funding allows them to broaden the reach of their operations within their mission, the leadership and staff are expected to be more deeply motivated and more thoroughly connected to the actual recipients of the services than government employees are likely to be.

The experiences in the last decades have however taught that the corporatist model of public service provision is not without inherent tensions. The process of acquiring, delivering and maintaining government contracts are burdensome to third sector organizations as they require potent doses of time, the contracts

38

come with high reporting and compliance requirements and as the contracting process may compromise the organization's independence (Lyons 2001: 141). Shergold (2009) for instance noted how third sector organizations sometimes have to deal with burdensome contractual obligations by a risk-averse public service. He also pointed out how government may be inclined towards micro management of their contract partners.

The requirement of working on government contracts is furthermore found to be a potent agent of change for organizations. Fowkes (2009: 35) reports from her experiences of organizational change in the Australian Job Network. She describes how some excellent staff left in disgust at the level of time they had to invest in government information systems. Fowkes also had to invest heavily in the knowledge and technology that was necessary to track job outcomes for clients and had to recruit people with business and sales backgrounds rather than welfare workers. These changes might be necessary in order to operate effectively in the new contract environment, but it could also mean that the organization becomes dependent (or, put negatively, 'addicted') to government funding and that the organization changes in a fundamental way. Shergold (2009), again, warns for mission creep: third sector organizations working for the government might forget or neglect their true missions (see also Cottle & Nolan 2009). Again Fowkes (2009: 34) provides a specific example, where participants in the Job Network were obliged to implement sanctions that they had been opposed to earlier.

2.4 Conclusion

The provision of public services in most advanced democracies in general, and in Australia and the Netherlands in particular, is different but not dissimilar. In many countries, public services are now provided by a plethora of organizations with quite different backgrounds and different formal and funding relations to the government. As a result, contemporary service provision is characterized by complexity and dispersion.

The variety of existing public service providers is displayed in the table below. The vertical dimension displays different types of public service providers on a scale from full public sector organizations (units in government departments) to typical third sector organizations temporarily contracted by governments. The horizontal dimension of the table displays the four most important organizational features on which the service providers can be either private or public. The two axes correspond in the sense that the organizations at the top of the vertical dimension are characterized by the public character of legal instrument, ownership, financing and staff. Organizations at the bottom of this vertical dimension are private organizations without public funding; essentially for-profit and non-profit organizations. The organizations at the bottom of the table are truly private organizations, they are not public service providers, and hence the cells in this part of the table have been highlighted in grey. The other organizations, the majority of types of public service providers, display mixed, and changing, patterns of public and private elements.

Table 2: Typology of public and third sector providers of public services

		Legal instrument	Ownership	Financing arrangement	Staff
PUBLIC	Unit or directory of central government	Public law	Public ownership	Tax collection	Civil servants
↑	Semi-autonomous public agency				
	Legally independent public agency				
	Private organization established or owned by the state				
	Third party governance: permanent service delivery by third sector organization				
↓	Contracting: temporary service delivery by third sector organization				
PRIVATE	'True' Third Sector Organization	Private law	Private ownership	Nonprofit distributing	Private (incl. volunteers)
	Private Enterprise			For profit distributing	Private

* Note: Table based on a combination of classifications by James & Van Thiel 2011; Coston 1998; Thynne 2003; Salamon & Anheier 1992.

The complex and dispersed nature of contemporary public service provision is relevant to our theme of mediatization for two main reasons. It is first of all relevant through *agency*: there are now many actors outside of central government providing services who are not directly controlled by the government and may (or may not) have the opportunity to use the media or be targeted by critical media. (Semi-) autonomous public service providers are potential *objects* of media attention and are potential *subjects* of media strategies.

Secondly, Cook (2005) has convincingly argued that the dispersion of political life and the public sector in the United States has been one of the main reasons why policy actors will start 'governing with the news' and be involved in 'government by publicity'. This implies that political actors integrate news making into the heart of their strategic operations. His suggestion implies that we may also find service providers in dispersed systems to be active media strategists. Where organizations integrate media management and the demands from their media environment in their operations, they become subject to mediatization. The next chapter will explore the issue in detail.

3. Mediatization and public services

"I start work at 3.30 or 4.30 in the morning. My media report should be ready at 7 in the morning, so I am doing 4 AM-shifts just to manage the media and prepare for a morning briefing on 7 am. They want to know what the issues are; how to respond. They like to know what is being said." (Director of Communications)

The pressure from the news media on politics and public organizations has grown substantially over the last decades (Cook 2005; Elmelund-Præstekær et al 2011; Strömbäck 2011; Mazzoleni & Schulz 1999; Kepplinger 2002). It is the product of a myriad of social, political, economic and technological changes. The media landscape has been transformed by the advent of new technologies, such as digital and social media. Journalistic professional attitudes have changed profoundly and journalists have struck increasingly critical tones. There have also been significant changes in the economy of news making, due to commercialization, concentration of media ownership and faltering sales of newspapers and advertisements. Simultaneously, politicians and political parties have had to learn to cope with ever more volatile voters in a context where public services and governments in general, have been subjected to severe criticism. The net effect of these seemingly disjointed trends has been that 'handling' the media has become an ever more important task for public service providers, particularly for the large organizations operating in politically salient domains. They have had to adapt their organizational structures and processes in order to internalize the demands from their news media environments and to translate these into their daily routines and practices. Public service providers have, in sum and to widely varying degrees, become mediatized.

This chapter will first explain how the media is understood and to what media this book is referring. It will be argued that the news media operate as a social institution whose method of influence is invoking change in other social institutions. The adaptation process in other organizations is defined as *mediatization*. We will subsequently advance an analytical framework with which the mediatization process of public organizations is traced. Its consequences – positive as well as negative – can be understood with the related concept of *media logic*.

3.1 The news media as an institution

Mediatization generally refers, as will be discussed at length below, to institutional adaptation to media. 'Media', however, may refer to a number of actors and institutions and subsequently refer to a number of different modes of influence.

According to Hardy (2008), 'media' may refer to at least four different types of phenomena. In its traditional and linguistically most correct sense, 'media' refers to the technologies with which people are able to communicate across time and space. In this sense, media refers to television, cable, telephone, broadband connections and the programs that allow social media to flourish, but also refers to earlier media innovations such as telegraph wires, homing pigeons, and smoke signals. Human messengers would also fit into this category, even though most real messengers would probably object to being listed among a set of technical devices.

To speak about media influence in this context is a form of technological determinism. It would imply that specific traits of the technical media with which people communicate have some form of influence on the content and or effects of the communication process. The archetypical example of this form of technological media influence is Kennedy and Nixon's televised campaign debate in 1960, where a healthy and smiling soon-to-be president Kennedy outshone the sweating and pale later-to-be president Nixon. The people who had followed the debate on the radio opined that Nixon had 'won' the debate, while the TV-audience was more impressed with Kennedy's performance (Druckman 2003). The example signals that the transmission of the same message through different media may have different effects on audiences (through the process of *priming*, Druckman concludes). It also most consequentially means that the style, speed and formats of public debates need to adjust themselves to the demands from newly emerging media. In the era of television, for instance, political actors needed to learn how to convey their messages in ever shorter sound bites (Patterson 2000a). As one experienced respondent in our research put it: "You should be able to speak intelligently and with details about any news issue for a maximum of three minutes". Note that this form of media influence does not point its finger at a villain: the possibly unwanted media influence is a consequence of the technical capacities and incapacities of the medium of transmission and the media's influence cannot be assigned to some person or organization.

The second sense of 'media' that Hardy (2008) discerns refers to the 'content': the sum total of all the messages that are transmitted through the different media, such as print, internet, radio, television, Facebook, etc. 'The media' in this sense refers to an ever-widening yet already immeasurably large field of communications. It is common to make distinctions between different journalistic genres in order to organize this incredible volume of available media content. Political and other social scientists naturally tend to limit their attention to the news media (and news on established policy actors in other journalistic formats, such as talk shows). The reason the apparently fragmented and disorganized stream of messages in different outlets is studied as a whole, is because news media research overwhelmingly found that media stories were showing strong signs of convergence in topics and formats. The same issues, the same formats, the same criteria, and the same incidents are repeatedly depicted in all different media. Timothy Crouse famously attributed this phenomenon to *pack journalism* in his 1973 book on agenda setting (Weaver et al 2004: 272).

When we speak about the influence of the media in this respect, we are talking about the large agenda-setting effect of repetitive media messages. A string of research endeavors has described how the media agenda affects the agendas of citizens and policy actors (see McCombs 2004 for an overview). The media are powerful in this sense to the effect that they influence what issues are seen as important by the public and, consequently, demand political attention. Media reporting also powerfully influences the specific frames in which issues are set and discussed. As Bernard Cohen stated in 1963: "News media may not be successful in telling people what to think, but they are stunningly successful in telling people what to think about" (McCombs 2004: 3). It is, again, a form of media influence without a real villain (although journalistic practice may be blamed). The repetition of more or less similar messages in the various media outlets propels issues from private agendas to public agendas and influences public policies. Journalists and editors are *collectively* responsible for this repetition, but it not a *concerted* repetition and it is the repetition itself that effectuates the media contents' influence.

The third meaning of media refers to the various *organizations* involved in the production process of the daily news. Media, then, refers to media corporations, news organizations, editorial teams, editorial boards, etc. The organizational level of the media is the perfect locus for piercing accusations of undue and undemocratic media influence. Here, the finger has been pointed at journalists being overtly leftist or apologetically uncritical of established authorities, or to editors favoring scandal and disruption above neutral, balanced and factual coverage, or to media corporations being more concerned with advertisements, market shares and economic profits than with the genuine journalistic mission of reporting *all the news that's fit to print*. Also, any or all of these organizations and persons are sometimes accused of political preferences or depicted as servants to some master's voice.

The fourth understanding of 'media' is as a social institution. Used in this sense, 'media' refers to a more or less coherent and independent social field of institutionalized norms, rules and modes of organizing and acting. It is in this fourth sense that we will use the term 'media' in this book.

There are a number of reasons why the news media should be properly understood as an *institution* (Cook 2005; Tiffen 1999; Hjarvard 2008). To begin with, the development of the news media in the past centuries went hand in hand with the evolution of specific forms of media regulation. Interestingly, many of these regulations were based on general civil rights to freedom of speech and the right of the citizen and voter to be informed about political decisions and administrative procedures in democracies. Nevertheless, the regulations specifically and directly benefited (or hampered) the class of news journalists; not the citizens proper. Most iconic in this respect is the institution of the press gallery in British Parliament in 1840, where only the journalists who were recognized as such by their peers were given a designated and enclosed space from which to operate. The press gallery symbolizes the advent of the news media as a recognized institution in democratic political systems. The press gallery is only one in a number of specific regulations shaping the news media as an independent political institution. The introduction of press cards, tax exemptions, and the fact that most courts will generally accept that journalists have a right to protect their sources, are all signs of the institutionalization of the media. These regulations all point in the same direction: they grant some citizens, journalists, privileged access to information, because this serves the civil rights of all citizens. It is an institution based on *general* civil rights on freedom of speech and information that are transformed into *specific* professional rights and obligations that favor – and sometimes constrain – those persons who can successfully claim to be journalists.

Furthermore, the news media can also be seen as an institution because that is how they are treated by most people and, according to the Thomas theorem, if people conceive of a situation in specific terms it is real in its consequences. The ease with which people speak about 'the media', and even speak about media in the singular, contributes to this perception of a coherent institution. The real consequences of this perception are that news media also have institutionalized organizational structures, professional norms, including shared understandings of what is newsworthy and what is not. These professional norms for what is newsworthy are often more relevant to the process of news-making than the personal opinions and values of a journalist. Interesting research among Dutch journalists for instance clarified that most journalists have indeed, as they have been repeatedly accused of, leftist political leanings. The recurring criticism is thus warranted. However, these personal political opinions were found not to affect their decisions on the newsworthiness or the contents of their news stories. A comparison between conservative and liberal journalists showed an overwhelming convergence in generalized professional style and norms, almost irrespective of their personal political preferences (Van Schuur & Vis 2002: 119-124; Deuze 2002: 70-71).

These shared professional norms are accompanied and reinforced by fixed production processes. Most news organizations are organized on a highly similar basis. They have adopted the same set of organizational structures and procedures and there is little variation in the ways in which they crank out their stories under the intertwined pressures from competition and deadlines. As a result, as described earlier, there is a large degree of convergence in the content and the formats of the news. Even more so, many journalists rely very much on other news outlets and the opinions of their peers in determining what stories to pursue and what line of enquiry to follow in their reporting. As a journalist described:

"I guess I read five papers every day. I get the Post at home and it's the first thing I see, so it shapes my impressions of what might be the flow of the news today. I look at how we might move the story farther down the road, beyond where it's already been" (quoted from Cook 2005: 79)

When we talk about the influence of the media as an institution, we are again chasing a phenomenon that is not attributable to specific persons or organizations. The institution exerts an influence on persons, organizations and other social institutions without any one person or organization being responsible. The process is related to Giddens' (1984) *structuration process*, in which institutional patterns and norms are the basis of social interactions that simultaneously replicate, confirm, modify and disperse these institutional patterns and norms. This process of institutional influence will be considered in the next section.

Before we proceed, a short note needs to be made. The above analysis explicitly referred to the old news media – and new news media – and not to social networks and the other forms of new media that are currently catching so much attention. Focusing on the old media begs the question of the relevance of this study. Why do we need to focus on the impact of antique media, such as newspapers, radio talk shows and the TV-news, in a time when everybody is exploring and exploiting the exciting new world of social media, or so it seems. For the organizations and people who are depicted in this book, however, the "antiquated" world of the news media is, even in lieu of twitter, wikinomics, and wikileaks, still the most important and consequential form of news media. The old news media provide access to a steady stream of vital data, information, and signals for policy actors. Admittedly, service providers are increasingly experimenting with new and social media in order to bring their messages across and to reach specific target audiences. Nevertheless, the reason almost all policy makers know about the existence and effectiveness of these new technical media in the first place is because they read about them in a newspaper or heard about them on television. For many policy makers, social media are currently to a large degree a mechanism that may help them to get (old) media attention and to do so on their own terms. Far from substituting the daily national news, for many policy makers the social media are currently rather a substitute for press releases and media conferences. As long as this remains the case, the news media remain the most important media for studying the mediatization of public service providers.

3.2 Mediatization

Mediatization is – just as similar concepts such as informatization, Europeanization or globalization – a meta-concept that refers to a large set of distinct but interrelated institutional changes (Krotz 2007: 257). Mediatization is a concept that is most often used by Germanic and Scandinavian authors and seems to be at odds with established linguistic rules, according to native speakers. It has for instance been dubbed as a 'clumsy neologism' (Livingstone 2009: 5). Mediatization is a specific variant of the more common term mediation. It is used distinctively to refer to specific instances of mediation, where the mediator is a medium that belongs to our species of media. It thus refers to specific forms of mediation, where media as mediators have a specific impact on the other actors or institutions. Not all accounts of mediatization specify to which media the author(s) refer. As there is a variety of media, mediatization may be invoked by different media, with different effects. A positive example which clearly explains to which media the author refers is Fortunati's (2005) *The Mediatization of the Net and Internetization of the Mass Media*. Following her example, it would be proper to speak of *newsmediatization* in this book, as it is to the news media that we will be referring. Newsmediatization, unfortunately, is an utterly unspeakable word, so for matters of convenience we will resort to the more conventional yet less precise term 'mediatization'.

In the political communication literature, Mazzoleni and Schulz' 'Mediatization of politics' (1999) is a landmark. Mazzoleni and Schulz explored how political processes, such as communicating, organizing and participating, had become more and more dependent on the (news) media in the course of the 1990s, and how political institutions were changing and adapting themselves to the external demands from the media. In their analysis, mediatization was a challenge to democracy itself, as it was thought to cause the decline of the model of political organization that was fundamental to modern liberal democracies (Mazzoleni & Schulz 1999: 247. See also Brants & Van Praag 2005). Their analysis was thus based on a pessimistic and declensionist perspective: political processes changed for the worse in response to the pressure from the media. Mediatization, however, is not necessarily a negative phenomenon (Schulz 2004; Hjarvard 2008: 114; Livingstone 2009). It rather denotes a *descriptive* concept that allows scholars to trace processes of institutional adaptation to media. As such it is an interesting concept, as it initially focuses on the media but commences to specify and analyze developments in other organizations or institutions in response to the media (Livingstone 2009: 5). In order to be useful as an analytical tool, it is then crucial to develop a concept that is descriptive, generalizable, and non-normative in nature (Strömbäck 2008: 230). The analysis of the process thus needs to be separated from the normative evaluation of the process.

On a fundamental level, mediatization is a relatively simple concept. It refers to all those situations where communication via mass media replaces other forms of communication or activities and to the ensuing adaptation of processes, rules, routines, and structures in order to do so effectively. Hjarvard (2008: 113) fittingly describes the process as follows:

"By the mediatization of society we understand the process whereby society to an increasing degree is submitted to, or becomes dependent on, the media and their logic. The (...) media have become *integrated* into the operations of other social institutions ..."

Mediatization has in recent years been used by a number of scholars in order to trace changes in practices, organizations and institutions in response to media-pressure. Mediatization is also a historicist concept, as it refers to changes over time. The impact of media on other institutions has been studied in numerous fields, but for our purposes, studies in political communication are obviously the most important. A very interesting article in this tradition is Kepplinger's (2002) analysis of the mediatization of German Parliament. He focused on the long term effects of increased media scrutiny on the activities of German MP's. He analyzed the activities of German MPs across time and investigated whether it was true that they were increasingly using their limited time on mediagenic activities, to the detriment of typical non-media events, such as the preparation of legislation. It is an important question, as, in the words of Arnold (2004: 12):

"If legislators observe that journalists convey little information about legislative activity beyond what legislators reveal in their press releases, they may focus their creative talents on writing press releases rather than making laws".

Kepplinger reassuringly found that German Parliament displayed a very stable pattern of law making activity. Simultaneously, however, he also found that all forms of *uttering statements*, a method of influence that is easy to make, has little consequences but easily attracts media attention, underwent very sharp increases over time. He concludes (2002: 984): "The growing number of articles triggered by statements gives the impression that a politician's work consists primarily of issuing statements". Other interesting analyses of mediatization on the meso level of political and administrative institutions include Rawolle (2005) on the Australian knowledge economy policies, Raupp (2005) on changes in organizational communication, Schrott & Spranger (2007) on political negotiations, Cottle (2006) on military and political conflicts, Hajer (2009) on policy making, Kunelius & Reunanen (2011) on elite decision making, Elmelund-Praestekjaer et al (2011) on MP-media interactions and Strömbäck (2011) on perceptions of the media's power.

The mediatization studies mentioned above all refer to the activities of political elites who are, in some ways, found to have been strongly affected by their media environments. This book follows the types of analyses made by these authors but must necessarily resort to different types of research, as mediatization will here refer to *organizational changes* that help public service providers to cope with the demands from their media-environments. In order to do so, it is important to look more closely at the concept of mediatization.

Mediatization is generally understood as a gradual process that evolves over time and can manifest itself in different ways. There are however some recurring elements in the definition. On the macro level of society in general, Strömbäck (2008: 236-240) has argued that the process consists of a sequential trajectory of four phases. In the first phase, media become important, or even the most important, sources of information in society in general or for specific organizations and individuals. In the second phase, media operate increasingly independent from governments and start operating on their own terms, through their own choices and according to their internal rules, procedures and routines. In this phase, news media become a separate institution in society. In the third phase, the media as an independent institution start affecting other social organizations and institutions. As organizations to some extent are dependent on the media (phase 1), and the media operate on the basis of its own, institutional logic (phase 2), organizations will need to adapt in order to be able to interact successfully with the media. This implies that they invest in their skills to operate the media. In this third phase, organizations for instance create a media-team that reports directly to the CEO, invest in media training or may even adapt their own routines to fit the schedules of journalists. In the fourth phase of mediatization, organizations internalize the external media rules and thus change in a fundamental way. For instance, journalists find colorful stories about the odd, incidental, maltreated patient more newsworthy than abstract stories about complex, structural transformations with a more general detrimental effect on all clients. Media need the human face. When organizations internalize this media rule, they shift their focus from structural problems to individual problems. Whether this is a good or a bad thing, is still a matter to be disputed. It nevertheless serves as an illustration of the logic of mediatization, where an organizations' internal understanding of what constitutes an important problem gives way to the media's external perspective. The example also illustrates that mediatization refers to very subtle and passive, yet incredibly powerful, forms of media influence.

The adaptation and internalization process consists, according to Schulz (2004: 88-89), of four elements. The first element is *extension*. This simply means that media allow persons and organizations to transcend the natural limits of communication. In effect, mediatization manifests itself through the increased intensity and the extension of patterns of communication across time and space. The unparalleled dispersion of communicative devices in the last century is, then, testimony to this first dimension of mediatization.

The second element in the definition is *substitution*. Mediatization further manifests itself when former unmediated activities transform into mediated activities. The literature provides many speaking examples of substitution: playing chess with a computer, for instance, is a nice example of mediatization; and playing chess against your opponent via an internet connection is another example. Actors in policy processes make frequent use of mediated messaging, where media communications substitute for 'normal', face-to-face communications. Addressing stakeholders via interviews in magazines, for instance, is now a common strategy, as is mobilizing political support via social networks and YouTube rather than via public speeches in front of the town hall and shaking hands in meetings. And texting your partner that you love her is, although arguably still a nice thing to do, an example where media-communications are a substitute for direct communications.

Amalgamation is the third element of the process of mediatization. It refers to the mingling of media-related activities with essentially non-media activities. The requirement of having to communicate effectively about policies, for instance, brings spokespersons of service providers into contact with the people who prepare the actual policies, and their activities may become connected. As a Dutch communications manager of a government department indicates he tells his staff: "It is our job to hinder the policy people in a friendly, but permanent way". In this example, the staff whose job it is to inform the media about evolving policies may start influencing those policies themselves; policy making and policy communication become mingled.

The last element, and the one that is of most important in a study of organizational mediatization, is *accommodation*. It refers to changes in organizational rules, structures and processes which are made especially for, or changed in order to, enable the organization to operate effectively in its media environment.

Hiring communications specialists is an obvious first step; repositioning and centralizing the media team within the organization is another step; training CEOs to handle the media and even select CEOs on their ability to do so is a further step; expecting policy advisors to carefully monitor the news and operate with permanent media awareness is still another step.

3.3 Mediatization of organizations

The four elements discussed above are helpful in the analysis of mediatization in *general*. This book, of course, is concerned with the analysis of mediatization in the specific situation of public organizations. This presupposes an analytical model of organization. We will base ourselves on what is considered a standard business model of an organization. This model distinguishes organizational inputs, from throughputs and outputs. Inputs, here, refer to the sources of information that public organizations exploit in order to scan their environments and to learn how to operate. The question is then, for instance, to what extent media-reports are important sources of information for public service providers and what organizational structures are used to accommodate this input? Throughputs refer to internal processes, on which the external media environment may or may not have an imprint. The question is for instance to what extent media-communication is integrated in policy processes and what organizational structures are used to accommodate this? Outputs refer to organizational interactions with the external environment, where organizations may, or may not, target the media. To what extent is media communication integrated into the execution of their core tasks and what are the organizational structures to accommodate this?

This standard business model of organization is arguably very basic and does not take into account the many, many!, existing and much more sophisticated theoretical models that have been developed in organization science (see Scott & Davis 2007; Rainey 2009). This is a deliberate choice which is necessary in order to contain the complexity of this project. The analysis of mediatization is already complex, as the research focuses on a number of different types of organizations. There are distinctions between public service providers with varying degrees of autonomy from the political administrative center and third sector organizations delivering public services. The comparability of the different cases requires us to use a relatively simple analytical model of organization to organize the research efforts and findings. Furthermore, the complexity of the mediatization concept necessitates a relatively simple model of organizations. There are a number of issues. First of all, mediatization is not a stable and irreversible process. As the media system changes, the levels and forms of organizational adaptation to news media may change over time. The forms in which mediatization manifests itself are also manifold. There are different ways to interact with mass media and to this end organizational routines may be adopted in different ways. The research confirmed this analysis, as we will see in the next chapters.

Mediatization is furthermore not a deterministic and unilinear process. Organizations have agency and are able to make their own strategic choices, albeit with the certainty that some strategies are more likely to fail or lead into reputational troubles than others. Some organizations are aggressive and are prone to invest in potentially risk-laden media-opportunities in order to bring their messages across. Other organizations act more defensively and would normally try to limit media encounters to the minimum and they only call for interactions in order to correct misinformation. No news is good news; these organizations are likely to think. The mediatization of organizations thus can take on different forms.

Finally, mediatization is not a one-way process. Public organizations and public policies adapt to the pressures and demands from the news media who in turn also respond to the peculiarities of public organizations and policies. The centralization and nationalization of public policies, for instance, has been one of the driving forces behind the gradual centralization of media systems.

Mediatization is all in all a complex process whose effects on organizations can best be studied on the basis of the simple and universalistic model of public organizations. In this book, three aspects of mediatization – the substitution of unmediated activities for mediated activities, the amalgamation of non-media related activities with media related activities and the accommodation of organizational structures and processes to these ends – have been investigated on the three levels of organizational process in the standard business model: inputs, throughputs and outputs. The mediatization of organizational inputs refers to the extent to which news stories are used as relevant sources of information for service providers. The mediatization of organizational throughputs refers to the extent to which intra-organizational processes are influenced by and adapted to the external media. The mediatization of organizational outputs, then, refers to the ways in which organizations integrate news-making (and news-avoidance, as we will see) into their actual service delivery.

3.4 Media logic

The elements above are helpful in analyzing processes of mediatization. When these concepts are used in the study of public organizations, the outcome will most probably be that all current organizations are at least to some degree mediatized and that some of them are more so than others. It would be very hard to find an organization shunning all forms of communications with the media (criminal organizations are the only examples that come to mind). The fact as such, thus, is perhaps not particularly interesting. The relevant follow up question is whether any of it *matters* (see Livingstone 2009: 10). Does mediatization really modify policy processes or public services, for instance, in ways that are important to our understanding or evaluation? Does mediatization for instance improve or impair the quality of public services? Does mediatization make public organizations more or less efficient? Does mediatization make organizations forget their true mission or does it, conversely, help them to actualize it in a media-saturated context? In short, what is needed, is some sort of a *normative* evaluative framework that accompanies the *descriptive* framework of mediatization.

The root for such an evaluation is already imbued in the concept. Mediatization has always been a theory that attempts to trace forms of institutional *colonization*. It assumes a *mutagenic effect* of the media on political life and policy processes (Mazzoleni & Schulz 1999: 249) where the rules of the media take precedence over the rules that used to reign.

The term *media logic* is often used to describe these rules and their effects and was introduced by Altheide and Snow (1979: 237-8). They stated that political communicators were forced to respond to the media's *rules, aims, production logics* and *constraints*. In this sense, news media determine what subjects are important to consider, they (help) create recognized experts and personalities and they become sources and guardians for official information. Members of policy institutions recognize the importance of obeying with these rules if they wish to reach their target audiences. Altheide and Snow (1979: 246) state:

> "In short, they present their own messages and images within the respectability and familiarity of media formats."

What, then, are the major characteristics of media logic? We shortly examine some of the most important rules, aims, production logics and constraints of the news media.

Rules

Journalists operate on the basis of a fundamental yet simultaneously highly ambiguous rule: 'newsworthiness'. Among the immeasurable number of daily events, journalists select a very limited and surprisingly coherent number of issues that lend themselves for a successful transformation into a news story. At a very general level, newsworthiness is about 'important' and 'interesting' news (Cook 2005: 5). Established authorities have a key access to 'importance', yet

54

they depend on journalists to understand them as 'interesting'. Communications professionals and journalists are both experts in the creative transformation of a myriad of barren facts and exclamations into an interesting story. To this end, journalists rely on established storytelling techniques and formats (Strömbäck 2008: 233). Among the consequential rules in media logic is the following, not exhaustive, list:

- The media prefer simple stories
- The media tend to repeat a limited number of recirculating *endless* stories
- The media seek personalized stories that display the human face
- The media tend to find polarization and conflict newsworthy
- The media often report in stereotypes
- The media (sort of) consider facts to be sacred
- The media (sort of) seek balanced reporting
- The media will often focus on established (news) authorities
- The media look for 'breaking news' and scoops
- The media tend to side with ordinary people against secretive large organizations, especially bureaucracies

Aims

The news media report on all the issues of public interest; the formal aim is to bring all important *and* interesting news to the public's attention. In this sense, the interests of news media and their news subjects largely converge, as most policy actors are actively trying to get their positive news published. Nevertheless, media and news subjects have *"overlapping interests but different purposes"* (Savage & Tiffen 2007: 84), because news media have other aims as well. For one thing, the media are a lot more interested in negative stories than the subjects in those stories naturally tend to be. The criterion of 'interesting news' furthermore emboldens journalists to focus on, and often exaggerate levels of, conflict, in order to make an issue as interesting as possible. This acclaimed tendency to overstate conflicts is further boosted by plain material considerations about making a profit or assuring reliable levels of government funding by selling more newspapers, attracting more viewers and listeners and, most importantly, attracting advertisers. Journalists finally serve their own and their organizations' professional status. They operate in a competitive environment, where large numbers of journalists are looking for the spectacular scoops that will parachute them above their peers. Professional competition is also multifaceted; there is competition between news outlets, newsbeats, bureaus and journalists for access, stories, resources and professional reputations. All of these aims have some form of impact on the selections the news media make and the frames they use when covering stories. All in all, the most relevant aims are:

- The media aim to bring important news
- The media aim to bring interesting news
- The media compete for advertisers, news consumers, and public funding
- The media aim to boost personal and organizational reputations and compete for scoops

Production logics

The daily news is a selection of the innumerable daily events, selected by journalists from the relatively limited yet still very large number of events brought to their attention. The news is then processed through specific organizational routines and practices. The question what the news is depends to a large degree on the news in other media. Journalists spend a lot of time listening, watching and scrolling through other (digital) media, and they also consult with reputed colleagues on their choices regarding selection and framing (Deuze 2002; Cook 2005). Journalists also tend to write or produce 'follow up' stories on earlier news. Furthermore, the content of the news is to a very large degree determined by *information subsidies*, such as staged press events and press releases by recognized news authorities such as politicians. Prior research suggested that more than half of the news stories are based on different types of information subsidies by authorities (McCombs 2004: 102-3, Weaver et al 2004: 270). Also, the work of producing news stories is carved up between different editorial teams and is organized around a set of pre-established themes. Some outlets also have special regional editions and regional editorial teams. This means that news selections to some degree are pre-established as there are more or less fixed news holes to be filled by pre-arranged editorial teams. In addition, editorial scarcity and the heavy competition for access to the news are important production logics. The main daily news on Dutch public television for instance lasts 25 minutes every day, almost irrespective of the daily events. The work of producing the daily news is finally organized through a series of deadlines that can be exploited by news sources seeking coverage. Important production logics of the media, thus, are:

- The media rely on news agencies
- The media rely on information subsidies
- The media rely on other media
- The media follow up on earlier stories
- The media work with a fixed editorial structure and in fixed teams
- The media have set newsholes and time to broadcast

56

- The media operate on deadlines
- The media compete for news

Constraints

The production of the daily news is in a number of ways heavily constrained. The technical media all enable and constrain stories in their own ways. For the daily news on television, for instance, interesting visuals and *talking heads* are important. In an interesting study, a foreign reporter described what an impossible time he had in providing a balance report about the conflict between Israel and the Palestinians. Israel claimed that the root of the problem was terror and there were ample opportunities to provide detailed and powerful footage of the horrendous effects of acts of terror. The Palestinians, on the other hand, claimed that the root of the problem was occupation and, although Luyendijk (2009) calculated that the occupation caused thrice as many casualties as terror, there were no comparably strong visual images available. As a result, he felt that it was just too difficult to provide a balanced overview of the positions of both parties to the conflict. Written media and the radio face similar constraints, and need their news subjects to be sufficiently eloquent. Furthermore, the media are of course heavily constrained in available time, reporters, their ability to check stories and the allocation of cameras and other equipment to produce the stories. Finally, journalists have very limited knowledge of most issues they report on. They rely heavily on existing public information and authoritative news sources for background information to their stories. The news is therefore usually somewhat biased towards the understandings of established authorities and tends to recirculate established frames for specific issues. This constraint has become ever more pressing in the past years, as editorial cut backs and a high level of turnover has made journalists scarcer, younger and less specialized than they were in the past. Important constraints, then, are:

- Media are limited in time, material, resources, access and localities
- Media work with technically constrained methods of transmission
- Media need their subjects to be able to present their side of the story (with a minimum of) eloquence
- Media needs visuals alongside stories
- Media produce stories with a limited numbers of journalists who (naturally) have limited knowledge of many issues

4. Media pressure on public service providers

The most important role of the media?

"Channeling public accountability of government / public administration. This is a vital role (for democracy)".

"Pointing out in an oversimplified way the "unfair" treatment by the service provider".

"Destructive".

The quotes above are some of the first associations participants in focus groups jotted down when asked to define the most important role of the news media for their organizations. Grossly a third of the respondents focused on the *opportunities* the media offer organizations to bring their message across (see chapter 7), a further third of the respondents focused on the *relationships* of their organizations via the media with their customers and the citizenry in general (see chapter 5, 6), and a final third of the respondents – some of their descriptions are depicted above – referred to a form of *pressure* that the media exert on the provision of public services. Some of those respondents, as the first one, described the media pressure in formal language and positive wordings. Some others, as in the last quotation, chose starker and more personal wordings. The responses seem to signal that *pressure* is the first association a number of people working for the providers of public services have.

The process of mediatization refers to forms of organizational adaptation to media pressure. As such, media pressure is a necessary precondition for mediatization. This chapter aims to understand the media pressure on public organizations. The chapter will first provide some details on the media coverage of public and third sector providers of public services in the United Kingdom, Australia and the Netherlands. It will be shown that the level of media coverage of service providers *collectively* is substantial, while the coverage of larger individual service providers exceeds the media coverage of many politicians. The chapter then proceeds with an analysis of the *content* of the news stories on service providers. The degree to which service providers are subjected to general trends in reporting, particularly the growing negativity and personalization of news, will be assessed. Finally, the chapter will discuss the subjective perceptions of media exposure and media pressure by respondents with senior positions in public service providers. The respondents almost universally felt that they were exposed to an exacting media environment, and they described the news media as an external force to which they needed to be alert, even in those situations where the actual levels of media coverage were not particularly high. Media pressure, thus, is not only caused by actual reporting but also by individual anticipation of potential reporting. In conjunction, the thrust of the presented 'evidence' here will be that at least the larger public service providers experience a considerable level of both real as well as psychological media pressure.

4.1 Substantial and dispersed media coverage

Many authors have noted that the news media have become increasingly important factors for organizations providing public services, claiming that most large organizations are confronted with a substantial pressure from the news media. Yet very few authors have actually investigated the issue empirically. This section will present different empirical findings on the levels of media reporting on public service providers.

The first 'piece of evidence' is the older Deacon and Monk (2001a; 2001b) research on the media and quasi non-governmental organizations (quango's) in Britain at the end of the nineteen-nineties. Their research focused on the media coverage of quangos, many former government agencies that were granted more autonomy in the course of the Blair-era. They showed that the level of media reporting on quango's had risen substantially in the course of the nineteen nineties (Deacon & Monk 2001b: 157). The increased media attention paralleled the policy process of separating the service providing agencies from central government departments. Furthermore, their analysis showed that a number of the larger agencies had a very high media presence, such as (naturally) the BBC, but also the Bank of England and the schools inspection (Deacon & Monk 2001b: 160). A further, more intensive investigation of all media in a short time span showed that the most mediagenic organizations in the UK were the subject of approximately 10 stories in the different media every day. Most organizations were also found to be active news monitors and they were actively trying to generate positive news.

This trend of growing media attention for public services has continued in the decade following Deacon and Monk's research, as is evidenced in figure 1 below. The figure depicts long term trends in media reporting in total numbers of stories on public service providers in England, Australia and the Netherlands in three quality newspapers for each country. The figure clearly shows that there is a large volume of stories on public service providers. More importantly, the figure also indicates that there seems to be a general increase in the levels of reporting on service providers over time. Interestingly, the patterns in reporting are remarkably similar and develop in similar patterns in the three countries, although it would be hard to explain this parallel reporting trend. The total number of stories in Australia is larger than in the Netherlands, although lower than in the UK for most of the years.

Figure 1: Trends in reporting on service providers in quality press[1]

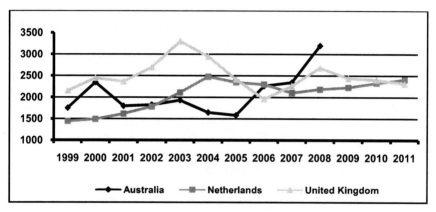

A second measure of the level of reporting comes from a comparison of media coverage of service providers with a sample of Dutch politicians. The comparison serves as a benchmark that allows us not only to answer the question how much media reporting there is, but also to establish whether this actually is *a lot*?

Politicians are the customary protagonists in the political news and they serve as a natural benchmark. Politicians, of course, receive varying levels of media attention. A small number of well-known politicians seem to be in constant interaction with the media, and they are incessantly covered on television, the internet, radio and in the press. Many other politicians, however, just plod on in relative anonymity. In order to assess whether the rising levels of reporting on service providers can actually be considered as a high level of reporting, the total number of all stories in all written news media on a list of large public service providers was compared to the total number of all stories in all written news media on all politicians from one political party, the PvdA (Dutch Labor). This list of politicians includes highly newsworthy politicians such as (then) party

---

1   Figure 1 covers 13 years for the UK and the Netherlands and only 10 years for Australia. There were technical problems in retrieving the data for the last three years; the findings were unfortunately unreliable.

leader, treasurer and vice-Prime Minister Bos, the parliamentary leader of the party and senior ministers, but also includes numerous fairly anonymous backbenchers. The average number of news stories on a selection of 28 large public service providers in one year was 1531, compared to 982 for all Labor politicians. Many of the large service providers, thus, received more media attention than the average MP! The most senior politicians featured far more prominently in the news than the most newsworthy service providers. Nevertheless even the least mediagenic of the large organizations still received more media attention than the average backbencher. This suggests that at least the large service providers are noticeable regulars in the news, not indistinguishable from the average politicians and more prominent than most backbenchers.

A third measure of the level of reporting on public services comes from an in-depth analysis of all (non-foreign) news stories in one Dutch quality newspaper (Volkskrant) during one month. In this period, 695 articles were coded and searched for public or third sector service providers. In total, 200 articles directly mentioned public or third sector service providers, something that equals 29 per cent of the total news stories. This number does not only include all the stories where public service providers feature as antagonists or protagonists in a story, but also includes the stories where service providers resume a less central role (say as deuterogamist or tritagonist). In some stories a spokesperson or CEO was quoted speaking about the organization and its services, in a large number of other stories journalists or politicians referred to service providers that could not respond themselves. The organizations 'figured' in other people's stories (Van der Steen et al 2010). Taken together, then, almost a third of the domestic news in a quality paper directly mentioned public service providers.

Public service providers are thus *collectively* important subjects in the news. On the level of single organizations, however, many organizations will have very little actual media experience. There are large differences in the numbers of stories published on different service providers. A number of repeat players feature in the news on a daily basis whereas the majority of relatively small organizations largely operate out of sight from the media. The table underneath provides an approximation of the variance in media reporting on a set of Australian public service providers, public as well as some of the renown large third sector organizations. The Reserve Bank of Australia was depicted in over 8000 news stories and more or less dwarfs the level of reporting on the other public services providers. Third sector organizations with large public contracts, such as Mission Australia and the Smith Family, are among the smaller recipients of media attention in this list of 28 large organizations.

Table 3: Total numbers of annual news stories for 28 Australian service providers

8295	Reserve Bank Australia	193	National Transport Commission
3000	Australian Competition and Consumer Commission	174	Australian Institute of Criminology
2962	Australian Bureau of Statistics	145	Food Standards Australia New Zealand
1794	Medicare	140	Landcom
1711	Centrelink	128	Smith Family
1378	Australian Taxation Office	113	Airservices Australia
1342	Bureau of Meteorology	92	Land and Water Australia
1210	National Park Service	81	Australian Energy Regulator
550	Australian Communications and Media Authority	79	Australian Fair Pay Commission
394	Austrade	61	Australian Council for the Arts
368	Australian Transport Safety Bureau	34	National Competition Council
303	Energy Australia	25	Australian Rail Track Corporation
259	Australian Research Rouncil	23	Crimtrac
256	Mission Australia	18	National Electricity Market Management Company

A further analysis in the Dutch context suggests that there are some *patterns* in the dispersion of media attention. To begin with, it seems that the media devote most attention to organizations providing direct services to the public, such as housing, community services, education or care. Some 70% of the stories lie within this category. In the Dutch case, the level of attention for third sector providers and public service providers was fairly even, both received around 50% of the attention. This however is a specifically Dutch finding, as most of the providers of for instance social housing, health care and education are private organizations working within a publicly regulated and financed environment.

A last indicator of the level of media pressure on public organizations comes from the small scale survey that was circulated among senior officials from service providers. The respondents were asked whether they (strongly) agreed or (strongly) disagreed with the propositions that their policy fields, and the organizations in their policy fields received a large degree of media attention. Their subjective perceptions of media attention were thus measured.

The figure below provides an overview of the answers from different groups of respondents to those two questions. Respondents have been clustered in three groups. The first, white, column refers to responses from people working for central government departments and service providers within those departments. The second, grey, column represents the answers from respondents working for (quasi-) autonomous public agencies and statutory authorities. The last, black,

63

column stands for the responses from people working for third sector organizations that deliver public services on either a permanent or a contract basis.

Responses have been measured on a 4-part scale, where the maximum score of '4' corresponds with strong agreement on a proposition, a '3' signals 'agreement', '2' is 'disagreement', and '1' is 'strong disagreement'. The neutral value in this – and the many similar figures that will follow in the course of this book – is '2,5'.

Figure 2: Subjective perceptions of media attention

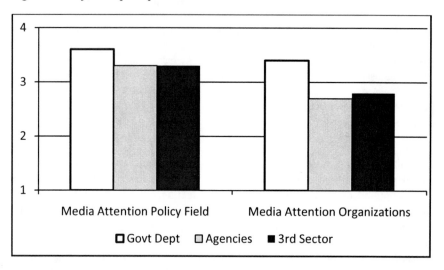

Figure 2 illustrates how most respondents overall perceive that there is a high level of media attention for their policy fields. Respondents in central government departments agreed more heartily with this proposition than respondents from agencies and third sector organizations. Nevertheless, almost all respondents at least agreed with the proposition, and the averages of 3,3 for agencies and third sector organizations are clearly above the 2,5-neutrality margin. It is interesting to see that the governmental respondents experienced higher levels of media reporting, considering that they generally work in the same policy fields as the other respondents. This probably suggests, as will be clarified as we move along, that perceptions of media pressure are higher when people work closer to the national government.

Figure 2 furthermore signifies that a large part of the media attention seems to be of generic nature rather than focused on specific organizations. As a result, the perceived media attention for organizations is significantly lower than for the policy field as such. It is little wonder, then, that the responses from departmental respondents are more outspoken than those from public and third sector service providers. A departmental respondent summed up this point as follows:

> "The system as a whole is open to attack. You will seldom see attacks on individual organizations, but often on the system, that's open to attacks"

Public service providers all in all collectively occupy a large niche – almost a third of the total number of news stories – in the news. Levels of reporting have been on the increase and the most newsworthy of these organizations are subjected to comparable levels of reporting as second tier politicians. This suggests that public service providers are, albeit somewhat inconspicuous, regulars in the daily news. As a result, they may also experience some of the *trends* in media reporting that contribute to the sense of media pressure: increasing negativity of news and increasing personalization of stories.

4.2 Neutrality, negativity and personalization

In public and academic debates about the contemporary state of the media, the growing negativity of the news has been criticized as well as the media's tendency to reconstruct difficult policy issues into partisan struggles between persons. The growing negativity of the news has for instance been investigated in historical analyses of the media coverage of American presidents. On a macro level, Patterson (2000b: 10) showed how each president since 1976 was subjected to more negative news than his predecessor. Where roughly a quarter of the news stories on president Kennedy in 1960 was negative, president Clinton had to deal with almost two thirds of negative news. And Congress was even worse of; over 80% of its coverage was negative. Patterson (2002a: 254) also described how media stories would focus more and more on politics as a *game,* a conflict or battle between persons, rather than parties or perspectives on public policy. On a micro level, Clayman & Heritage (2002) showed how journalistic questioning has become increasingly adversarial in the years between the Eisenhower and Reagan presidencies. In their interesting study they analyzed the questioning techniques used by journalists during press conferences. They showed how journalists were making their questions ever more adversarial and "tough", by cascading questions, introducing questions with factual statements, and more assertiveness and directness.

Earlier research has suggested that these trends in reporting, the negativity and personalization, extend beyond politicians to governmental agencies and service providers. Patterson (2002a; b) for instance also notes how important federal agencies are equally exposed to negative news. And the trend of personalization has also been noticed for some large service providers whose CEOs developed into real media personalities (see Mulgan 2002; Brenchley 2003). And Deacon and Monk's (2001a; b) research suggested that some 80% of the general news stories on quango's for instance had a negative tone, although most stories on specific policy decisions were cast in more neutral terms.

This last distinction, between the breaking news type of stories on the front pages and the routine news on evolving policies and decision making processes is of great importance, also for our more recent data on the media pressure on service providers. The front page stories suggest that news coverage has indeed become highly critical and negative. However, when the total volume of the daily news is taken into consideration, it turns out that the stories on service providers have only to a limited extent become critical and personalized.

The personalization of stories has been investigated in a content analysis of news stories. All news stories in all media were collected for the list of 56 large service providers. All stories were subsequently checked for use of the name of the organization's director or CEO. Personalization, then, implies that journalists find it somehow important to mention the name of the highest ranking person, representing the organization, in stories. The findings suggest that some CEOs become real media personalities to the point where they are usually mentioned in news stories on their organizations, while most CEOs fail to make it into the news (or: succeed to evade the news). Only two Dutch CEOs (representing the national Bank and the publicly owned national airport) had a very large media presence in stories on their organizations as well as in other forms of personal media attention. The Australian research saw a few more examples of personalization, where the CEOs of four organizations, the Australian Taxation Office, the Reserve Bank, the Australian Competition & Consumer Commission, and Mission Australia, developed into media personalities. Most of the other CEOs received only scant, or even no, personal mentions in the media.

The examples exemplify a general trend in reporting: journalists tend to look for established authorities and known 'performers' when they construct their stories and broadcasts. They work from a limited base of established authorities and, evidently, only some of the CEOs from public service providers are included – and *want* to be included – in this list. And once they are established as 'interesting' and 'performing' news subjects, it is quite likely that they will be recalled time and again.

The findings for the second trend, the growing negativity of news stories, are somewhat similar to those for personalization. At a first glance, an analysis of all the stories in the domestic sections of quality newspapers shows that the media indeed bring far more negative than positive news. There are actually almost thrice as many negative stories as there are positive stories. However, when we only focus on the 'treatment' of public service providers, data set 3 indicates that there is also a large fond of thoroughly 'neutral' news, as Deacon & Monk (2001a, b) found earlier. The analysis showed that 14% of the stories was positive, 40% was negative and 45% was neutral. The neutral stories particularly focused on organizations with a regulatory task or providing data and research. The 'real' public service providers, the organizations providing direct services to people in health care, education, and social housing, were the subjects of most of the negative attention but also of almost all of the positive stories. This pattern repeats itself when we look at the public and third sector divide. Public organizations featured most often in neutral stories, whereas third sector organizations seem to enter the news in more extreme senses in either positive or negative stories.

A further analysis of the positive and negative stories reveals an interesting pattern: organizations are given much room in news stories to reap the benefits of positive news. In a disproportionate number of the positive news stories, the CEO or some other spokesperson is quoted directly in the story. However, when organizations are portrayed in negative stories, it is relatively rare for them to have the opportunity to answer in person and directly to allegations and criticisms. This is no doubt a consequence of the repetitive nature of the news. There are more stories across a longer period of time on negative issues than on positive issues. In the investigated period, a number of service providers lived through scandals that were cross referenced in follow-up stories. The organizations probably had the opportunity to provide answers when the first stories in these chains of reporting appeared, but in subsequent stories, the scandal as such was an established fact that evidently needed no balanced form of reporting. In that sense, public service providers (and other news sources) are vulnerable in the news as established interpretations of events will resurface over and over again without the organization having an opportunity to challenge the established interpretation.

This dependence and vulnerability is further underlined by the tendency of politicians to comment on public service providers who can find it hard to challenge or cross a politician. Particularly the Dutch third sector service providers experience this situation: in some 77% of the stories, politicians are quoted with comments on the quality of services or organizational problems. Third sector service providers are thus potential subjects of political spin in the news. Challenging political interpretations can be an uphill battle for service providers, being criticized in the news media is then a liability that is not easily corrected.

To conclude, the level of negativity and personalization of the news on public service providers seems to be lower than for politicians. In comparison, it is interesting to note that service providers feature in large numbers of thoroughly *neutral* stories, which are often not more than annotated organizational press releases. The neutral stories recap factual developments in service provision. In their ability to enter the news with factual stories, service providers seem to have a specific *asset*. However, once they find themselves the subjects of critical reporting on large incidents, the organizations are particularly exposed and vulnerable. They are often not given the opportunity to argue their case, they are criticized and even attacked by sometimes scornful politicians, and they are given little room to defend themselves.

4.3 Experiences of media pressure

How do senior officials experience the existing media pressure on public services? Answers to this question are varied of course. Initially, most respondents point out that the media are potentially important in a democratic system, the respondents stress, that the media can be important sources of information for their work and that the media's presence and modus operandi are simply a fact of life. "The media is simply a part of our job", one Dutch respondent noted. And another respondent adds: "I think it is important that a watchdog is watching over us, as we are a large service provider". And a third respondent added: "It is a real issue in a democracy. Democracy depends on an informed public, so the media has a very real impact."

These positive descriptions of the role of the media *in theory* were however almost always followed by more critical qualifications of the ways they enact their role *in practice*. The media are theoretically important, most respondents would note, but everyday practice falls well short of the glorious theoretical ideal type. The figure below provides a first insight into some recurring criticisms. The figure, again, shows how the assessment of the role of the media is more intense and critical the closer to central government respondents are working.

Figure 3: Assessments of the quality of the media

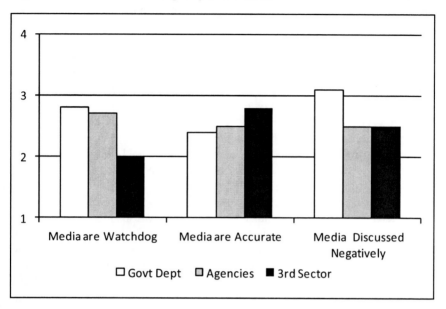

The figure above first of all shows whether respondents thought the media were a de facto positive watchdog in the public sector. The average scores on this question were marginally positive; most people thus seemed to feel that the media to some degree live up to their important role as watchdogs (see Norris 2013) of public services and policies. Nevertheless, quite a few individual respondents answered negatively to the question. And it was also striking that particularly respondents from third sector service providers had a negative view on the role of the media and did not feel that the media were living up to their role. One respondent from a third sector organization for instance stated:

> "The government, people in public administration, third sector people, they all largely aim at improving society. But that is not the motivation of journalists and that is the failure of the system."

This respondent, and some of the others, pointed out that journalists and people working for public services work towards different ends. Where public services work towards social goals, the intentions of the media, and most explicitly talk back radio hosts, are questioned. "They have no moral point. They just look for weak points, and they attack and off they go", a respondent notes, whereas another respondent adds: "They are not driving the agenda anywhere in particular. They just drive it".

Opinions differ on the issue of whether this moral background matters or not. On the issue of *accuracy*, however, most respondents spoke unisono. As figure 3 above indicates, the accuracy of media coverage is contested by almost all respondents. Across the board, the respondents feel that the quality of the coverage is not too bad. However, this is not always an accomplishment of the journalists. To begin with, the *resources* of journalists are seriously challenged. One respondent for instance recalls: "The correspondent is twenty-three and she always wants it tomorrow. There is no time to put it in context. We get lots of coverage but there is no balance". The respondents point at a decline in expertise in journalism, the lack of contextual knowledge of journalists, the limited number of people hired, the high turnover, and the pressures of the 24-hour news cycle. As a result, there is a lot of coverage that is one sided or only to a limited degree based on existing facts. This seems to be a challenge as well, however, as most of the facts can be filled in by service providers or government departments; it is thus an element that can be handled pragmatically. A respondent from a highly media sensitive organization noted: "Whenever we have a story, the reporting will even itself out. About a quarter will get the story wrong in one sense and another quarter will get it wrong in the other direction. So on balance, it is not too bad." But even when the facts are correct, the story is always presented in a specific frame, and typified in headlines which are often added in the final instance. This is a major source of irritation. One respondent sums up the approach in a shorthand: "There are basically two types of news stories: Isn't it wonderful or isn't it a shame?". Journalists present their stories in specific frames and prefabricated forms which make them focus on specific aspects of stories and force them to leave out many other aspects (Scheufele & Tewksbury 2007; Entman 2003). As such, most stories lack the type of context people in public services and government find most important. It is a matter of focus: in news stories a specific story of individual tragedy or triumph is usually presented, whereas service providers are looking at more complex systems and large categories of beneficiaries of services. When the story points out something shameful, public sector agents may have a hard time correcting the image. One respondent stated:

> "They work on the model of Samson and Goliath. And the baddies are circulated between government, business or a swanky individual. It's always the little guy, or the individual, against an irresponsive but powerful opponent. It's a set format, and one in three stories is like that."

Most of the respondents had the strong sense that news reporting had become ever more restless and fast. This is causing journalists to make mistakes and to publish and broadcast incomplete, factually incorrect or heavily biased stories. The pressure on news production has of course grown, with the advent of the internet, talk back radio and the proliferation of ever more commercial television that will pick up on scandals from the public sector. Whether it has actually decreased the quality of reporting is difficult to tell. However, most respondents were quite convinced that this was the case, so it is at least their experience of media pressure. A respondent notes: "I'm probably more cautious about the quality [of reporting] than ten years ago."

The media as an external factor for public services does exert real pressure on people in public organizations. Figure 3 above showed how most people at least some of the time speak negatively about the media at work. This suggests that the media are a real source of pressure for them. For some people, the pressure is very real and they state that they sometimes reach their work in a state of precautionary anxiety. A respondent notes: "You wake up and you see the paper and you think 'here we go'. You're ready for a day of preps and calls that decides your day." Another senior respondent adds: "You sometimes go to work with the stress: 'what's going to happen today?'". Some respondents feel it is a negative pressure, as media stories sometimes crucify the programs they have been working on for five years or may totally change their priorities for the day. The massive character of the news – aptly described in the literature with the term *pack journalism* – and the fact that negative news seems to stick whereas the many positive stories are easily forgotten – contribute to this experience of real media pressure.

This pressure is not only felt within large public organizations, respondents also feel that negative reporting can have a large and undue influence on the communities for which they work. The pressure of the media can be very intense and is difficult to manage, even for trained media performers and even worse so for a local school principal caught up in a sudden media storm. During one of the focus groups, the following string of observations on the issue was made by respondents eerily filling in on each other:

R1: "Very often, school principals or other individuals, they're not prepared for the intensity of public scrutiny and feel immensely vulnerable."
R2: "It's a screaming media pack."
R3: "Sometimes even people spit at you."
R2: "At first, after the first time with big news in the papers, I had to lie down because of the incredible effect of public scrutiny."
R1: "There is a lot of genuine anger at that, also because media never say sorry. They may leave a school community traumatized for years."

The difficulty comes from the different perspectives on *relevance* between media and public services. Public services deal in general programs for groups of constituents; the media focus on individual cases where someone has experienced something horrible (or wonderful). Spokespersons defending the benefits of general programs in news items on horrible experiences by individuals face an uphill battle. A person defending an organization or program in the face of incidental, individual tragedy will hardly ever surface on top in a debate. Public service providers are strongly affected by critical media coverage, it could lead to changes or even the termination of their programs, and they don't feel they have a fair chance to redress criticisms. As a result, some – by no means all – of the respondents voice negative or even cynical views on the quality of the press and the influence it exerts on public policies. And the positively minded respondents nevertheless concede that it takes a lot of carefulness and tact to handle the media.

In its strongest form, the problem of how to handle potential negative stories is described in the longer example (below) provided by a director of communications of an Australian government department that provides public services:

> "The sensationalized media: you can't train people to go there. The level of skill you need to do well on such a program, there is hardly any staff I would allow to appear on such a program. Even the most skilled person will have problems in a 10 minute segment. For instance, there is a 10 minute part on one of our programs. Even if you have all the data proving it's a good program, they may have one person with a heart ripping story, tears etc. They don't check the veracity of the story, but it's a good story, so they send it anyhow, for nine minutes. And then you have like thirty seconds to respond. If you don't put someone on the program who is incredibly media skilled, you will just get crucified on the program. And it's probably not worth it to go anyway."

4.4 Media pressure in sum

Public services overall occupy a substantial niche in the newshole of a quarter to a third of all of the media stories. Many of those stories (40%) are negative and point at failures in programs or focus on individuals who are supposedly harassed or maltreated by irresponsive public service providers. Some service providers feature in the news on a daily basis, whereas many others hardly ever manage to pass the gatekeepers to the news. Many small organizations never make it into the news, unless by a chance "good luck story" or a sudden explosion of media attention for an incident. For the larger public service providers, however, the media are an ever present outside force that can be used strategically but is nevertheless also a source of pressure. A major aspect of the pressure is the fact that media coverage can be very influential and also very demanding on a psychological level, yet for public organizations they are indispensable. It necessitates public organizations to engage in public exchanges on the core of their work in media formats that are set in unfavorable terms. "We try to change the rules", one respondent notes, "but we are beaten at it all the time."

When we look at the differences in media pressure between public and third sector providers, two observations stand out for now. The first observation is that the large third sector service providers in our research do not differ significantly from public service providers. They also experience media pressure, some of the larger organizations are subjects to equal numbers of news stories to the second tier public service providers. The only real difference seems to be the *tones* of the stories: third sector organizations appear in more outspoken good news or bad news stories, whereas public organizations also have a large share of neutral stories.

The second observation is that there is a real difference in the answers between core governmental departments and the other public or third sector respondents. Both the intensity of media coverage as well as the negative evaluation of its consequences, is more outspoken in the center of government than at more peripheral service providers. This finding may signal both the larger level of reporting in real terms as well as a larger inability to handle the pressure. Central government departments are more dependent on their political superiors in terms of handling the media. In addition, as they deal in policies-in-general, it may be that it is more difficult for them to respond to negative stories on particular cases, as "the system as a hole is open to attack".

5. Mediatization of organizational inputs

The most important role of the media?

"Representation of issues that are important to citizens and will take root in society."

"Create a space where public service policy and action can be examined and informed."

"Help disseminate the message when policies change and to gauge reactions to these changes."

The quotes above are some of the first associations of participants in focus groups when asked what the most important role of the media is. Roughly a third of the respondents referred to the media as a source of valuable information, thus as an *input* for their organization. The previous chapter described and sought to understand the media pressure on public service providers; this chapter will focus on public service providers as *news consumers*. It will answer questions such as: How much news do participants digest, to what ends and with what means? We will look at the importance of media information for senior employees and executives in public service provision, the structures that *accommodate* media monitoring and the ways in which media information *substitutes* for other forms of information or *amalgamates* non-media activities with media activities. This will help us in the end to answer the question to what extent the informational inputs of public service providers have become mediatized.

5.1 'The pictures in our head'

Public service organizations operate in a complex social reality, constituted by social processes, economic developments, legal structures and politico-administrative turbulence. Strategic decision making within those organizations is predicated on various forms of information and knowledge. Public service providers operate with skilled professionals and with a specific information- and knowledge structure that allows them to tap and trace relevant changes in the external world. Public service providers are also among the most important 'fact-producing' institutions of society and generally sit on a wealth of archival data. Public service providers are, thus, generally well-endowed with data and information; the media are generally not a part of this information structure. However, because of the complexity and unpredictability of their environments, public service providers may turn to media reports in order to learn about relevant external developments.

In political processes such as voting, the news media have been found to be incredibly important enablers, as almost all voters will know almost everything they know about policies through media reports, either directly or through hearsay. Walter Lippman famously wrote in 1922 that the world we deal with politically is "out of reach, out of sight, out of touch" (see McCombs 2004: 1). As a consequence, most people make their political decisions on the basis of the 'pictures in their head' of the 'world outside'. Media reports are extremely important to this end as they are the most important bases for most people's judgments on most political issues. For public service providers, however, this should theoretically not be the case. Public organizations are often large bureaucracies, possessing a wealth of resources with which they are able to find, accumulate and digest high levels of information on policy issues and social problems. Third sector organizations often have fewer resources, but as community-based organizations they can be expected to possess first rate and first-hand knowledge of their field and their clients. For the pictures in their head of the world outside, public and third sector service providers thus theoretically don't need to rely on media stories. Nevertheless, the respondents in this research were almost without exception found to be heavy media users and generally thought it imperative to know the news, even where the news was often not in meaningful ways *new* to them.

The figure below provides a gross overview of the levels of news consumption by respondents. The figure displays answers to the questions whether respondents believed that it was important for their line of work to follow the news closely, and to the question whether they generally found media coverage informative. The long and the short of it is that all respondents thought it was professionally important to know what 'happened' in the media and they also generally, although considerably less so, thought that the news was informative to them. In addition, in line with the findings in the previous chapter, the figure indicates that the media are more important for people in the center of government departments than for those working for more autonomous service providers. Nevertheless, all respondents indicated that they were heavy media users, as was also found in earlier research (Cook, 2005; Deacon & Monk 2001a).

Figure 4: Public service providers as news consumers

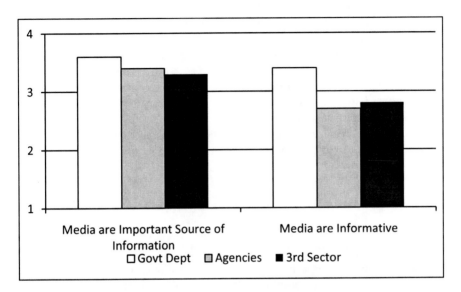

It will hardly come as a surprise that the people working for societal causes in public service organizations find it important to read newspapers and watch the news. It is probably a matter of *self-selection* to begin with: people aspiring to these types of jobs are likely to be habitual news consumers. The more interesting question is the follow up question: *why* do public service providers make a point of 'knowing the news'?

"It would be silly not to", one respondent in one of the focus groups replied to the question if, and why, they professionally followed closely what was on in the media. The other participants in the room hummed in recognition. Without exception, all respondents indicated that it was essential and important, for one or more of a variety of reasons, to be aware of the relevant news. They overall felt that it was an established fact that people in public services are expected to know what the news is and to be sensitive to the risks and opportunities news stories might have. A senior respondent from a politically sensitive agency for instance noted:

> "You start your day by reading the papers. Because you know that what's in there will be important. This has been taking more and more time. It is also expected that civil servants read the papers, know what the stories are, etcetera."

Another respondent from a public service provider added in a similar vein: "I read five, six papers every day. I believe it is insatiable, we're expected to know everything that happens in our portfolio". The closer people work to the executive level of the organization, and the more strongly a field is politicized, the stronger this expectation of knowing the news seems to be.

'Knowing the news' by watching, listening and reading media is to some extent a personal habit of the respondents and is considered to be an issue of individual responsibility by their employers. It has however also been subject to forms of organizational accommodation that allow organizations to organize media inputs into their organizations. Almost all researched organizations had invested in structures and processes with which they could systematically monitor the news and with which they were able to coordinate the diffusion of contents of, insights from and responses to the news.

5.2 Accommodation: multiple forms of monitoring

"We wake up every morning to an email at 4.30 that gives you a rundown of what's up, of every story that is on." (CEO in media sensitive agency)

For senior people in large public service organizations, the news media are a relentless and permanent companion. When they work in mediagenic organizations, the news is often the last thing they check before they go to bed and it may well be the reason that they wake up hours later. People in public services have a 'natural' appetite for the news and for public issues, of course. They would not stop reading the papers should they lose their job. Their natural appetite for the news receives a further boost by a string of accommodative structures and processes that monitor the news, and analyze and distribute the outcomes within their organizations.

The first accommodative structure is the *communications department* of the organization. Most large organizations will have communications or media people and, as one of its directors describes, following up on the media is a large part of what they actually do. They will often have the radio running all day, some organizations have hourly transcripts of the radio, and some people will always be busy looking at the newspapers, watching TV or scrolling through web pages on the internet. In addition, some large organizations indicate that they have media contact all through the day and that this allows them to trace what is 'happening' in the media. Some other respondents add that, as the "news junkies" they are, they will "listen a lot to radio, read papers and look at the TV and browse through the headlines on the internet". They will often pick up on things and whoever sees it will warn his or her colleagues.

The media people "do not sit back and wait for the news to come"; they actively follow the production of the news and will be alert at the time the papers are printed. Large organizations and government departments will have people "on duty", analyzing the papers as they are set, being warned by editorial teams if "anything comes up" and already preparing responses while most people are smugly asleep. As a rule, organizations feel that they should know the news in advance and be prepared to respond. "In my former job", one of the respondents recalls, "we actually set out the gear [for the press] the night before, because we already knew it would come the next day".

In addition to the internal monitoring service by the communications department, at least almost all large Australian service providers have invested in external media monitoring services (see also Ester 2007). The monitoring service steadily reports on developments in the news, sending round clippings and reports at reliable intervals of sometimes one per hour. The monitoring service will scan all media for references to specific search words, the name of the organization or service that is provided or will measure the media-impact of campaigns or decisions. If we conceive of media reporting as an emergent yet fractured storyline, then external media monitors allow organizations to gauge and analyze the evolving stories. The monitoring services produce large stacks of analyses that provide "snapshots" of what the "touchstone issues" are.

Some of the larger organizations add that they make thematic or periodical analyses of the media-monitors that they receive. Organizations then look for trends in reporting, sources of dissatisfaction or success, or associations with related issues. The organizations will also monitor all media requests, will sometimes analyze trends in media requests, and will monitor the effects of specific target actions. "We produce a sort of 'travel journey' of the media team", a respondent notes. Furthermore, once the CEO or another spokesperson appears in the media, analyses are often made of his or her performance, although the outcomes of these assessments are shared less liberally within their organizations.

The three types of monitoring activities described above all emanate in documentation in the form of clippings, email alerts, reports and conclusions that are actively sent through the organization. It is a process of warning, signaling and dissemination. This process primarily aims at the executive level of the organization, but many more people are included in the stream of information as "we want our people to know what the news is". A respondent notes: "As a civil servant, I started every day with the media monitor by Rehame, who operated on a million dollar contract. The report would set the agenda of the day". Many others have the same experience. The basic difference between the organizations is the time at which the report on the media is produced. People in the media team often have contact with the media until late at night and very early in the morning. For many other people and the organization's executives, the first reports are sent in at 6 or 7 in the morning for media-sensitive organizations and until 10 for less media sensitive organizations. In early meetings the organization decides whether or not to respond or act on the news.

For people in executive positions, the stream of information from the different monitoring mechanisms can be quite absorbing. A regional director of a highly media sensitive organization recalls:

> "We have two different monitors on the phone. One on the state level that warns on news stories, the other gives more contextual information to the news. I read them both every morning; we have three to five media emergencies every week. Anything happening near one of our centers, whether or not it has anything to do with us or whether or not the person even is a client, is news. So I start the day at 6.30 in the morning with the monitor and also finish my day that way. If you'd respond to everything that is passing, it would be a fulltime job."

The previous chapter clarified that the level of media pressure varies considerably between different organizations. In addition, some of the third sector service providers are considerably smaller than many of the public service providers. This naturally restricts both their inclination to monitor the news as well as their ability to set of resources to this end. As one of the small third sector service providers indicated: "We run on the smell of an oily rag, so we will certainly not waste money on media monitoring." Nevertheless, even in those organizations where media-monitoring was equipped far less professionally than in the larger organizations, respondents still expressed that it was important to monitor the media. Very often they then focused on specialized media, legal documentation, advocacy magazines, professional publications, or whatever would be constitutive of their mission.

5.3 Substitution and amalgamation: signaling

Public service providers all digest large doses of media information. What, then, are the reasons to focus considerable time and scarce resources on the media and to what extent is this proof of mediatization, in the sense of substitution (substituting non-media information for media information) and amalgamation (relating non-media activities to the media)?

During the interviews and focus groups, respondents outlined a number of reasons and ends to which they used media stories and media monitoring. Some of those reasons related to the core objectives of their organization. Media monitoring was then used as a commodity that provided insight into the social issues they were dealing with professionally, the effects of their services, or innovative methods of service provision. In these instances, one could argue that media information serves as a *substitute* for non-media information, as organizations are theoretically cognizant of their own programs and the needs of their clients. The minor part of the responses fell into this category. The larger part of the responses indicated that people use media monitors as devices with which to scan their strategic environment. In this sense it is a form of *amalgamation*, as external relations and internal priorities become connected to media reporting.

Substitution

Senior officials in public service organizations could in principle learn many things about the impact and context of their own work from the news. Media stories could in principle provide valuable information on social developments, arising problems, organizational effectiveness, etc. Most respondents however indicate that they find media coverage only marginally helpful in this sense. "Most of the stuff they report on is actually historic", a senior respondent states. The stories as such are often not considered to be too informative, as "we will usually know beforehand what will hit the media". In addition: "It is often informative but unreliable" and "much of it is white noise, it doesn't really matter." A senior respondent even uses a little test: "Whenever people complain about the impact of the media, I always ask them to name yesterday's issues. They will generally remember very few of them, if any at all, anyhow".

After qualifying their responses in this way, many respondents nevertheless conceded that media reporting actually was of some importance to their work. The respondents mentioned the following seven reasons.

Media coverage can first of all provide valuable *community-information*. A few respondents indicated how they were sometimes alerted to developments in the local communities for which they worked through media stories. The specific framing of the media story, and the focus on the individual, needs to be removed from the story, they stated, but underneath the specific media-frames, the stories sometimes contain valuable information on the communities for which they work. "The stories sometimes verify your own perception of what goes on in a community. It is like a barometer."

Customer satisfaction is a second issue that can be grasped via media stories. One respondent notes how media stories sometimes alert them to specific complaints by individual customers that may later resurface in the formal complaint procedures. In this sense, negative stories on services can serve as early warning systems of customer dissatisfaction, particularly in large organizations that operate from multiple localities.

A third issue for which the news media can be important is *implementation-information*. In fragmented service environments, with local branches or cooperating networks of service providing organizations, developments in implementation sometimes only become manifest through media reporting. Much of the reporting is scandalized and sensationalized, the respondents claim, but they will nevertheless sometimes learn about implementation issues through the media. The media are, as one respondent notes, "a heuristic device that helps us to trace issues."

Solution-information is the fourth form of substitution. For innovative organizations, media reporting sometimes provides clues to potential new solutions and approaches. Journalists are geared towards new and interesting developments and they may sometimes simply be the first to identify an approach at the local level or in a foreign country that is interesting and promising. One respondent for instance notes how (s)he sometimes learns about interesting community approaches elsewhere from media stories.

Regulatory information is the fifth form of substitution. Some organizations operating in very specific legal or regulatory frameworks will sometimes learn from the news about new developments in regulation or about legal interpretations by courts of specific tracts in acts. For public organizations proving legal assistance, specialized media can be important to this end.

A sixth issue that is mentioned is *external (international) trends*. The work of some organizations is strongly affected by international developments which may be hard to monitor properly. Respondents from these organizations indicate how they often learn about relevant developments from the media rather than from their formal notification and intelligence systems. A respondent working for an organization with a health care focus stated: "Media reports from Mexico on swine flu for instance came days before we saw it formally through international reporting." Another respondent from a large public organization added in a similar vein: "We have a deliberate process to look at media in other countries for signals".

Policy frame information is the final category of issues that can be informed through media stories. Many public policies are set in specific frames. As a senior respondent notes: "If there is a big reform, the political party will more or less take over and *focusgroup* the issue. It is 'handed across' then. The process very much focuses on the wording". The specific wording in a policy domain, then, becomes important for public and third sector service providers who want to maintain, renew or acquire contracts for services. A respondent from the third sector for instance noted how (s)he would follow the news more intently after entering a partnership with government, as (s)he felt it had become much more important "to get the words right".

These are the seven areas where at least some respondents felt they regularly received bits of valuable information or intelligence from the news media. These areas all pertain to the hearts of the operations and programs of public service providers. In that sense, it can be understood as cases of substitution, as media information is used in addition to, or sometimes in preference to, their primary sources of information. It is a long list of issues, which could be relevant to many public services, but should however not convey the erroneous conclusion that most respondents generally found media stories hugely important for their work. This was explicitly not the case. Telling is the fact that all respondents in one of the focus groups actually started to laugh when they were asked whether they sometimes learnt something valuable for their work from the media. A respondent stated: "We wouldn't expect newspapers to bring something we didn't know. We would be horrified." Nevertheless, the media were important for the jobs of almost all of them, but mostly for strategic rather than for substantive reasons.

Amalgamation

The importance of media reporting is that it provides insights into the political-strategic environment in which public services are delivered. Public service provision is to an important degree dependent on a politico-administrative context in which a host of policy actors and organizations are or may become influential. In this context, media stories may provide important *clues* and *signals* to the intentions and moves of other important agents. It is a form of advanced Kremlinology: tracing strategic developments in advanced and complex governance settings. All respondents in our research referred to this signaling quality of media reports. One respondent for instance noted: "A media-conflict is highly informative, as it tells you the boundaries of issues and the positions of actors". Another respondent noted how (s)he would always read specialized media where interest groups sometimes "fought, so we know what we can expect".

The media are thus seen as a source of information on the moves and intentions of all other parties – politicians, competitors, legislators, citizens, interest groups, important specialists – who might be important to the organization or to the provision of a service. People find it important to know about the behaviors of the others, as they "want to be on the front foot", as a respondent clarifies. It enables organizations to prepare and coordinate responses, to brief staffers and CEOs, and sometimes prepare replies or follow up activities. In government departments it is a well-known fact that media reporting to a large degree predicts political questions in Parliament. Some people claim that they already start the preparation of their answers to Parliament immediately after the appearance of a story. This anticipation effect is even stronger in the long term perspective. "The media is a driver for policy", a respondent says, "so we just need to know what's in the media. We wouldn't say so to a new staffer, but it is the way it works". The repetitive nature of media reporting, where highly similar stories appear again and again across the different media, is important in this respect. Many people indicate how they look for trends in reporting that might be important for future service delivery.

There is a general psychological theory stipulating that people rely more on media reporting when their 'need for orientation' is higher. The need for orientation increases under conditions of relevance and uncertainty (McCombs 2004). This holds true for most of the involved actors in the provision of public services. They operate in politically and economically unstable environments, where many parties might help them to or prevent them from attaining their goals. Media stories are then potential clues.

All of the above examples describe how public service providers scan their boundaries through media reporting, which can be considered as forms of amalgamation, as it clarifies how the organization's future orientation and external relations are partly operationalized through the media.

It is finally interesting to note how respondents here are generally more defensive than offensive when talking about the media. There is no a priori reason why media reporting shouldn't alert them to as many opportunities as to threats. However, the concern for damage to the reputation of the brand, message control and crisis prevention, is far more dominant in the responses than potential benefits and opportunities. A senior respondent from a third sector service provider sums this defensive approach up curtly: "Good issue management prevents you from having to do crisis management." And a respondent from a public organization adds: "They expect people at my level to be their eyes and ears. You have to see trends and risks and be very proactive in feedback."

The risk-aversity aspect of media monitoring also became prevalent in the survey: all respondents from all organizations agreed that it was highly important for their line of work to be able to see reputational- and communication risks in advance. On a 4-part scale, the answers ranged from a very high average of 3,8 for respondents from government departments to the somewhat more moderate 3,5 for public and third sector providers of public services. Their responses suggest that there is more to be lost than to be gained through unanticipated news stories. The news stories will seldom open up new opportunities but will often threaten to dent or complicate policies and programs. As a result, media monitoring is often a precautionary measure. A respondent describes the general reaction to media stories nicely as follows: "The government department often reacts as a porcupine, highly risk averse".

5.4 Mediatization of inputs in sum

Public service providers are heavy media users, and media stories are important tesserae in the informational mosaic with which organizations work. People in public services actually seem to learn and benefit from reading, listening or watching the media, even though quite a few of the respondents were reluctant to admit so. However, it is very often not the *content* of the message itself that is valued by the respondents, but it rather is the strategic information that manifests itself through media coverage. The hidden stories within or behind media reports are important, as they provide clues to the future behavior of important stakeholders and may teach service providers how their own moves fit in their larger strategic environment. Media coverage in that sense is quite like the weather forecast or market capitalizations. They are often not valued for what they *are* but for what they might foreclose about future important events. Media reporting is used much like signaling in economic theory (Cook 2005: 197). In a divided governance system, where different actors are involved in decision making, regulation and the provision of services, and where responses from citizens and interest groups are sometimes consequential, the different stakeholders try to learn about each other's intentions and moves through the signals hidden in media stories.

Media stories are important forms of input for all types of service providers, irrespective of whether they have a public or a third sector status. There are however differences between organizations. The main difference in responses is not the distinction between public and third sector service providers; the so-called proximity to political decision centers is of far greater importance. Respondents from all organizations suggested that media stories were an important source of information to them, but the 'closer' one comes to the political decision centers, the more professionally media monitoring is accommodated and the more intensely people scan media stories for important strategic signals.

The 'timing' of media alerts is a neat indicator for the different weights organizations attach to the news as an input. Media-sensitive organizations, such as government departments and some public service providers, receive their first media reports before the start of a normal working day (reportedly between 4.30 and 6 o'clock in the morning) and may provide hourly transcripts and reports on the media-tide to their senior officials. Many of the other less media-sensitive organizations in service provision 'did' the media somewhere between 8 and 12 in the morning and only receive media clippings once a day.

The table below provides an overview of the most important dimensions of the mediatization of organizational inputs that have been discussed in this chapter

Table 4: Overview mediatization organizational inputs

Accommodation	Substitution	Amalgamation
<ul><li>Communications department</li><li>Internal media monitoring</li><li>External monitoring services</li><li>Thematic and periodical media analyses</li><li>Impact assessment of campaigns, announcements, proposals.</li><li>Permanent media contact</li><li>Monitoring of all media requests</li></ul>	Media provide information on:<ul><li>Community-developments</li><li>Customer satisfaction</li><li>Implementation</li><li>Innovations and new approaches</li><li>Regulatory developments</li><li>External (international) trends</li><li>Policy frames</li></ul>	<ul><li>Future orientation</li><li>Signaling: media stories convey clues on 'moves' stakeholders</li><li>Strategic scanning</li><li>Strategic decision making</li></ul>

6. Mediatization of Organizational Throughputs

"Sometimes organizations can get hung up on what's on in the media. A notorious talk radio host was (very often) very vocal about our organization. I said to the CEO one day: 'Imagine if you just turn him of. Imagine that you as an executive – and the minister as well – don't listen. What's going to happen? Just turn it off. Don't listen. By listening so much, you hand them the power. What is the worst that's going to happen? You are still running your business. You still need to know who your stakeholders are and their concerns.'

I think there's way too much attention sometimes. And it takes the focus of the business. Takes the focus of the business. They are too hung up on the personal thoughts of radio talk show hosts. It can change policy. ... We don't really know what the community thinks of us. My idea and the CEOs idea of what the community thinks of us is what we hear in the media. But maybe they don't reflect the feeling of the community. ... I think we lose focus when we listen to the media too much." (Chief Communications officer of large public service provider).

The quote above – somewhat surprisingly formulated by a communications officer – sums up the fear that some external observers have repeatedly expressed in the past decades: public organizations may become so absorbed by the media spectacle around them that it takes their attention away from their main duties. Executives and the staff of public service organizations may, according to the concerned outsiders and the respondent above, lose perspective on their real priorities in the face of media pressure. It is a true form of mediatization, where the external media logic colonizes and subjugates the original organizational routines and logics; it is the *mutagenic* effect of media logic (Mazzoleni & Schulz 1999: 249).

This chapter will trace the mediatization of organizational processes – throughputs – in public service providers. In many ways this intermediate level – between inputs and outputs – is the most difficult level to assess as a researcher. It is plainly difficult to grasp what is going on inside the different offices of public service organizations. And yet it is the most important potential locus of mediatization. Should internal processes within public service providers really and in a strong sense be attuned to the external media demands, the organizations would have truly lost much of their autonomy to the outside media reality.

This chapter will clarify some of the ways in which organizational processes within public service providers are substantially affected by the media environment, and show that organizational throughputs are significantly affected in a number of important ways. However, our findings do not support the negative and alarmed opinion expressed in the above quotation. The findings will rather underscore the quotation underneath, spoken by a senior civil servant: "Generally, I don't think about the media very much as a civil servant. But, in many respects, they play a very distinctive role in my daily work".

6.1 The shadow of the news

Are the media important in organizational throughputs, i.e. in organizational processes? The figure below provides a first impression of some of the different ways in which public service providers respond to their media environments. The figure describes how the media have an influence on organizational processes within different types of organizations. The figure reports on three questions asked in the questionnaire that relate to the role of the media in internal processes. Respondents were asked a) whether they often discussed media reports in meetings, b) whether their executives were highly media sensitive, and c) whether media communication was central to their organization's strategies. As figure 6 below visualizes, their responses overall stressed the importance of the media in internal processes, as the respondents more than readily agreed or strongly agreed with the survey statements.

Figure 5: Importance media on organizational level

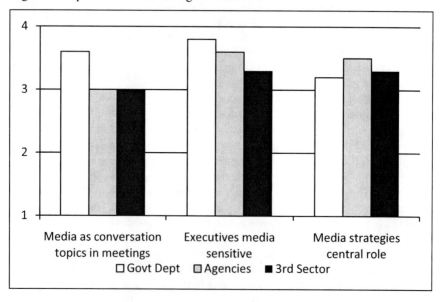

The first bundle in the graph shows how all respondents agreed that media stories are a topic that is regularly discussed in meetings with internal staff and external stakeholders. This suggests that media reporting is generally found to be salient; it is an important part of the strategic environment in which all service providers operate. The finding is probably not particularly surprising. It nevertheless provides a clear indication of the permanent presence of the external media in internal processes. This was most strongly the case for employees of central government departments (with an average score of 3,6 on a 4-part scale) and slightly less so for the other types of organizations.

The second bundle in the graph depicts the most significant part of this figure. It refers to the assessment of non-executive employees of the media sensitivity of their executives. Their general answer was that the executives were highly sensitive to media stories, more so in the Netherlands than in Australia and more so in central government departments than in third sector organizations. But even there, the average answer of 3,3 indicates a strong support for the statement that executives are always very sensitive about media stories. It is a finding that is fully in line with the literature on branding and reputations management.

The third bundle refers to the most fundamental of the three questions: is the communication policy of the organization fully integrated into their central policy processes? The original Dutch formulation of this question was, harking back to the term used by a government communications committee (so-called Wallage Commission), whether communication was "in the heart of policy processes". Again, all respondents answered affirmatively or strongly affirmative to this proposition. All respondents from the different organizations felt that communication had become a central facet in their general strategies. In this sense, policy processes can truly be said to have become mediatized; as communication has apparently become integrated into central organizational processes and strategies. The fact that the executives are highly alert to media stories and media opportunities further underscores the point.

On the organizational level, the three questions above sketched a picture of a high level of mediatization of processes within public service providers. The follow up question is, then, whether this has meaningful and important implications for the daily routines and practices of the non-media staff? The long and the short of it is 'yes', but to varying degrees.

Figure 6 below provides an overview of three indicators that sketch a widely varied picture, where the experiences in central government departments – where activities closely mirror the media environment – really stand out in contrast to the experiences in third sector service providers, where the respondents report a relative autonomy vis a vis media coverage.

The figure clarifies that the media pressure is highest in central government departments, where the daily events in the media have a direct impact on the activities of non-media employees. The respondents generally report to be very alert to media stories (3,5), acknowledge that media stories often influence their daily activities (3,3) and even that media stories might more generally change one's priorities (3,3). Processes within central government departments thus closely vibrate with the external media events.

Figure 6: Importance media on personal level

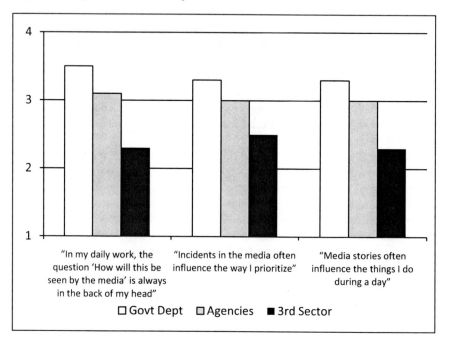

The picture in figure 6 is grossly similar for public service providers within and outside of government departments, although to a slightly lower degree. The third sector respondents, however, sketch a hugely divergent picture. The respondents from third sector organizations responded more or less neutrally to all three questions, implying that their internal processes are not severely affected by the daily media reporting. The finding suggests that third sector organizations do not need to worry so much about the impacts of daily media reports as people in central government do, no doubt in part because the level of reporting on their work is much lower. Third sector organizations do follow and use the media, however, but seem to be less affected by the daily news than other service providers are. They are perhaps more in the driver's seat in their relation to the media; for them it is a critical external asset that can be managed rather than an external force that always threatens to impinge upon one's daily work.

6.2 Accommodation: "You just don't put anything, anywhere, that could end up in the wrong place"

The introduction of media teams in organizations is the most visible form of accommodation to the media. 'Visible', however, should not be taken too directly, as it is often difficult to see from the outside which persons and parts of organizations are actively involved with the media. It is a name tag not always distributed too clearly. Ward (2007) has described how there can be different types of organizational units that are primarily concerned with the media. He distinguishes between the 'media minders' in the personal staff of ministers (and other executives, we could add) who operate a permanent hotline with the news media. Then there are 'media units' that are installed to create the favorable press coverage most public organizations aspire to, and there are 'public affairs' sections that more generally foster beneficial external relations. Finally, there has been an increase in whole-of-government coordination within states, across federations, and also in the relationships with external service providers, which has a strong flavor of media- and message control. The respondents in this research generally conferred to this view.

Overall, the level of public resources and the number of people put into media-work has been on the increase both in the US (Cook 2005: 135-6) as in Australia (Barker 2007: 126) and the Netherlands (Prenger et al 2011). Not only has the number of 'media'-people increased over time, their work has also become more central within the organizational processes. Figure 5 already noted this in our cases. In most public service organizations – both public as well as from the third sector – dealing with media and communications was an important aspect of the workload of the executive team, and the media team was situated centrally and just one tier lower in the organizational pyramid. On the organizational level, the accommodation of media-work thus placed it on a high central level. With the odd exception, all respondents noted that their organization had some form of a *media code of conduct*. It even lead to an occupational transformation within public organizations, as one of the respondents noted with some exaggeration: "More and more politicians and advisers used to work in the media. In the past, the civil service used to consist of lawyers, you know".

The centrality of media teams is probably an expression of the felt necessity to be able to cope effectively and swiftly with media incidents, risks and opportunities. In addition, however, it also signifies that the media can be an important external factor that assists executives whenever they want to make important changes within their organization. One respondent for instance indicated in one of the focus groups – to the nodded and hummed approval of many of the others – that the media can be very helpful external forces with which to perfect internal affairs. (S)he stated:

> "Often there are issues where we say: 'We wait for something to happen (in the media, TS), so we can justify changing things.' We all have to prioritize, so sometimes it takes a splash of the water to be changed, and sometimes the media can be helpful here."

For newly appointed or elected executives in particular, the media team and the communications policy are some of the readily and easily available tools with which they can bring about visible changes to their organizations. Some executives from large organizations for instance describe how they would spend a lot of time talking to the press during organizational transformations, as they found that this would boost the morale of their staff. In addition, they experienced that it was often convenient to use the press in order to get a message across to all of their employees. In a number of the interviews, executives referred to an important or even foundational organizational transformation they had initiated. In all of these cases, the media team and the media policy were crucial elements in that transformation. One respondent from a third sector organization providing social services described how (s)he brought in an external media team as a first step in a much larger restructuring process. One executive from a public service provider told a similar story:

> "In the past, there were some problems with (...). The media really surged for our organization. And we didn't have a very cogent media policy. We did have a media officer, but it was all low key stuff. And suddenly, all channels wanted us to appear on TV. (...) It was very savage, nothing nice about it. They just wanted to have blood, bodies, heads on pikes, so they say. So we had to be media savvy very fast. The previous chairman wasn't media trained. They didn't come across quite well. It was a period of prolonged torture, just torture. Our reputation got a real batter, every day again. (...) So the very first decision I made after coming here was saying that the only people who could speak to the media, on the record and of the record, were the members of the executive team."

Organizational processes are thus accommodated to the media, and the media policy and media team are potential tools for executive change management. In addition, however, there are also other and less deliberate or desirable forms of adaptation of throughputs in public service providers. One of the very specific forms of adaptation is that media pressure – accompanied by freedom of information clauses – affects how people communicate within the public sector and particularly inside governments. There is a general trend, for instance noted by Barker (2007: 130), that civil servants will quickly learn not to put things in emails as they may be FOI'ed. The respondents in this research all conferred to this view. They stated that the requests for information came in "increasingly and often by journalists". One respondent noted how (s)he always reminded people "what they put in emails, in letters or reports. Always be aware it might be FOI-ed." New staff is "briefed on how to document things as they may well arrive in the public arena." The general line is, according to one respondent, thus: "You just don't put anything, anywhere, you know, that could end up in the wrong place". People may be asked: "How is it going to look on the front page of the tabloid, you know?" As a result, personal comments are filed less and less often. People are very cautious, they feel they have to, and "start ringing each other a bit more often to let of steam". The cautiousness not only refers to what's documented in and on memo's and reports, but may also refer to more virtual types of information. Respondents from a Dutch service provider – providing the type of services not all recipients are too happy to receive, to put it mildly – for instance noted how personal information of their frontline workers, including photo's, contact details and their home addresses, was sometimes published on the internet, with potentially serious consequences for their private lives. In an Australian case, a respondent refers to communications via mobile phone equipment that is sometimes tapped by individuals. The respondent noted: "They have to be careful how they tell their colleagues about responses that can be heard, because it could end up [in public] and be defamatory."

These are all *personal* mechanisms with which employees ward of the potential threat of public disclosure of intentionally classified information. Earlier research has in addition pointed to some *institutional* mechanisms with which public organizations check the potentially negative effects of media publications, such as restrictive interpretations of the law, acts of omission and other administrative routines that allow public services information control (Roberts 2005 : 6; see Snell 2002). The respondents in our research additionally indicated a few more options. One option would be to change periodical reporting in order to decrease the number of media storms. One organization for instance recalls that they used to provide two reviews a year that always attracted a lot of media attention and a lot of critical discussion. In response to this, they decided to limit themselves to just one review a year. In a Dutch case a similar solution is mentioned: a service provider with a large, varied and controversial portfolio decided to stop publishing individual reports on its diverse activities but chose to integrate everything into just one major report, as this substantially lowered the level of discussion, reporting and criticism. The point is not that the organizations behave more secretive, but rather that they use deliberate *timing* and *crowding* techniques to lower the levels of criticism and media reporting. The same recipe should be followed in crisis management, one of the communications officers notes: organizations should establish all damaging facts as soon as possible and then "shovel it out at once". This ascertains a large burst of negative publicity but also abbreviates the length of the media-episode as the chances of follow-up stories shrink. Another respondent adds that, following the increased critical attention by the news media, they now "publish more, so they (the journalists) don't have to seek and think: 'There must be a reason why it is buried'."

All in all, there seems to be a considerable level of accommodation to the external media within organizational processes. Handling the media requires substantial resources and they are usually located at a central level within public service providers. In addition, respondents report how some of their daily routines, particularly in light of the freedom of information concerns, have changed. The follow up question for now is: in what ways does this affect essentially non-media activities in organizations and, thus, lead to amalgamation?

6.3 Amalgamation: anticipation & centralization

The activities of non-media people in public organizations are influenced by and amalgamated with media activities. In addition, media pressure exerts some influence on strategic relationships within public service providers and between service providers and governments.

When we start on the personal level, there are a large number of ways in which the activities of the non-media staff in public service providers are amalgamated with media activities. To begin with, grossly half of our non-media respondents indicate that they have had some form of *media training* in the past; slightly more often so in the Netherlands than in Australia. There was no significant difference here between public and third sector service providers. More generally, senior people are generally expected to be *alert* to the media, and mostly so the people who work close to central government. One respondent notes that this is a general disposition that people acquire on their way up in the hierarchy: "The more senior you become, the more alert to media you become. Junior people often don't see the point; they feel it takes them of their work." Another feature that accompanies people during their professional ascent is that their *days start earlier and earlier* because of the media. 'Handling the media' often means rising and starting early, where one respondent from a highly mediatized organization reports that its media strategy of the day is often decided at the fourth consecutive meeting on the issue at 9.15 in the morning. By 4.30 in the morning, the news of the day would have been brought forward already via email, blackberry, text message or i-phone. It is usually not the case that the email- or blackberry alert summons people into action, it is rather so that people just need to be aware of the news and to be aware of the potential effects of stories.

The most general *attitudinal* effect of the media is to infuse employees with sensitivity for the news and a sense of cautiousness, bordering on risk aversion, in handling and observing the media. As one respondent noted: "Part of what you do [regarding the media] is working out where it's going to go. It's risk assessment". People generally need to be cautious and cognizant of the media "out there", and organizations can sometimes become very shy and risk avoiding. Particularly central government departments may sometimes react sharply negative to the potential threats in news stories. Civil servants strive to isolate their ministers from potential reputational damage and political problems that may ensue from specific stories. So they respond defensively, also because "95% of the news stories are positive and there is no problem, but it's the five percent of damaging stories that can be very influential."

The operational translation of organizational cautiousness is: *anticipation.* Respondents almost unisono reported that even potential media stories on their organizations usually lead to heated activities. People spoke about "preempting responses to potential or actual media inquiries", about preparing files with data and responses even during the weekends when (potential) media coverage rung the alarm bells, and "checking and correcting factual information in media stories". The executive of a large but media-shy Australian public organization for instance indicated how they corrected about one issue a month that was misinterpreted by the media. The Dutch minister Donner (2004) once argued that the role of the media and the civil service had reversed. Ideally, it would be that journalists checked and corrected the information published by the government and the civil service. Increasingly, however, according to his view, civil servants were checking and correcting the stories published by the media. The respondents in this research did perhaps not share his overall assessment of the situation, they nevertheless made it abundantly clear that news stories always lead to a lot of checking and sometimes correcting within government departments, public service providers and third sector organizations.

The 'facts' are highly important in these instances, people feel, so all sails are set to get hold of the facts. The advice is to "Verify and get hold of the facts, then disclose everything you're certain about." The traditional expression for journalism is that facts are sacred and opinions are free, so public organizations respond in style by providing and checking facts. In addition, the more conspirative souls also investigate the origin of negative stories. As one executive resumes: "We are always good at researching. Why? Where does it (the negative news story, TS) come from? Why does it come? Ninety percent of the time we are able to anticipate". The anticipation then should lead to a swift, factually correct, balanced and convincing response by the organization, as a respondent underneath clarifies:

> "The moment something comes out, someone is already preparing the talking points, if they haven't done it the day before already. And in the course of the day I get the talking points in the mail, with all answers to all possible media questions. They are sent out to everybody who might talk to the media in the course of the day. The Prime minister's Office (PM&C) drives the process; they are pretty controlling and very directing".

The non-media staff is often involved in the 'production' of facts for media responses, yet they are generally not involved as spokespersons, in particular not when there is a risk of a media storm. Non-media staff is however involved in two different capacities. First of all they may sometimes be called upon to *background* journalists on issues, partly because they know more about the details of a policy or service than the communication team does, and partly because communications officers are generally not trusted too much by journalists. Another form of amalgamation is that some respondents note how they are encouraged to write their reports and policy advises in a style that fits with modern media demands. An executive respondent notes for instance that the minister should be able to speak with details about any news issue intelligently for about three minutes. Another respond adds: "We should write our reports in lines that could be told in eight seconds."

On a more structural level, and this follows logically from the observations above, mediatization translates itself in intra- and inter-organizational centralization. In order to operate effectively in the often critical and sometimes unpredictable media environment, organizations make every possible effort to keep *message control*. "There is just so much more information available", one respondent notes, "so you need to manage it". And a communications officer adds: "Our work is that we manage the message. That's what we do all day." The recipes for message control consists of different ingredients, but generally at least encompasses the restriction of media contact to the happy few of well-trained media performers. The focus group of third sector organizations for instance agreed upon this premise in very outspoken terms:

Respondent 1:   "The fewer people engage with the media the better."
Respondent 2:   "We have a very clear policy: 'thou shalt not speak to media'. Everything goes through the media people. If you get a phone call [from a journalist], you ring the media person."
Respondent 3:   "None of my staff will talk to the media."
Respondent 1:   "It could go all over the place. But as we're partially a local organization, we can't control all media contacts. So we prepare the people as we can't restrict them. We provide talking points, and q and a's".

Keeping message control thus means restricting the number of people with media contacts, and streamlining the messages and information that are disclosed. It has been noted earlier in the literature, that civil servants in particular have become less and less accessible for journalists, even for providing background information only. Barker (2007: 127) and Ester (2007: 104) describe how employees may even be afraid to talk to the media, because of the potential internal repercussions and more generally the "current pressurized time". Ester also notes the extensive reporting-back mechanisms that have been installed and that allow governments to keep track of all media inquiries.

Restricting the number of people with formal or informal media contacts leads to a higher demand for organizational coordination of communications that simultaneously elevates the communications policies and media officers to the top of their organizational pyramids. This leads to some tensions between the PR people and the non-media people. An experienced public official for instance describes how this tension consists of some elements: the PR people are geared towards getting out good messages and may be less sensitive about important organizational and role boundaries. They additionally want all information immediately, whereas public organizations often feel they need time to trace and check reliable data. An experienced communications officer noted the same tension, however phrased slightly different: "The departments invariably respond too slowly". Furthermore, the PR people, in the words again of the experienced public official:

"[They] simplify and politicize. As a civil servant you accept the second but the first is a problem you have to handle, because the message should be accurate. So very often, our role is to scrutinize press releases. They should be accurate, not only factually accurate but the general picture should also be accurate from a good policy perspective. You just have to constrain the enthusiasm of ministerial press advisors."

The ensuing 'professional struggle' between media- and non-media people can work out in different directions, very often shaped by the priorities the executives attach to external communications. A Dutch executive for instance recollected in a similar vein as the above quotation how (s)he put a lot of energy in discouraging the communications team from venturing on new publicity campaigns. In other organizations, however, the policy of 'any news is good news' seems to be nurtured and their media people accordingly call many of the shots.

Part of the professional struggle relates to the question of who may bring the good and bad news and who needs to answer to critical questions from journalists. One respondent felt that "Politicians want the media irrespective of the story." However, most of the other respondents rather sensed it was a more complex consideration:

"The minister is very ambitious. (S)he always looks for issues to run. They are continuously looking for opportunities to bring out a story. But if there is half a chance of running badly, (s)he wants someone else to take it."

Bad news is often brought by the department or a service provider while ministers always want to run the positive stories, most respondents argue. And ministers have the first pick of all possible stories. A media person from a public service provider states: "We only get to do good news when the news needs to go out and the minister is somehow not available". And another adds: "Most departments only get second or third rate media." An experienced respondent notes how the public service in the past would take care of public service issues in the media, whereas the minister would concentrate on the political issues only, "but in this room I would say that more and more this is reversed. If it is a political issue with a bad outcome, the public service media team will be sent in. And if it's a public service issue with a good outcome, the minister will be there to reap the benefits."

In addition to the intra-organizational centralization through mediatization, there is also an external centralization, where the lines between the Prime Minister's office and the departments, and between departments and third sector and public service providers, have been tightened over time. "This is a major issue", one of the respondents notes. Particularly when election time draws closer, there seems to be a particularly strong incentive to centralize and strengthen the coordination of public communication. "It is seen as risk management", a spokesperson from a public service provider notes, "it is very often not about getting a message across". The centralization extends well beyond the formal boundaries of the government. In the field of education, for instance, respondents note how local school principals are obliged to contact the educations department before they are allowed to speak to the media. And third sector organizations are also drawn into the realm of government, when they work on contracts and wish to speak to the media about the subject. They sometimes need approval to issue press releases, may have clauses in their contracts that restrict them in speaking about the policies in public, and they often need to use the government's logos in all communications. In addition, some third sector organizations feel "they (the government) want to share the glory". It is not surprising that governments seek to minimize the negative publicity that may emanate from external parties they are funding. Nevertheless, as Maddison & Hamilton (2007) have argued, this can be a major issue for third sector organizations, whose capacity for advocacy work is seriously impaired (see also Kelly 2007: 1017).

The centralization of (the coordination of) public communication sometimes spills over into the loss of organizational autonomy of service providers. Macintosh (2007) for instance describes how the organizational autonomy of at least four Australian statutory authorities has been challenged and curbed in order to press them towards more conformity. This was done through strategic appointments, by taking away powers or redesigning the governance model of organizations. During the focus groups, people were often very outspoken about appointments, stating for instance: "There is absolutely no doubt in my mind that some people have not been reappointed on account of what they said in the media on the government". Some executives had the same experience. One executive with a high media profile who sometimes challenged the government, said: "I was appointed for X years, so they couldn't do much. So I continued on [with a high media presence], thinking this will be the end of it." And another outspoken executive recalls: "There was a push for control from somewhere else. They were really after our organization. They brought in someone new and in the end: they 'caught' us". It is impossible to substantiate these claims here on the basis of our research. Nevertheless, it is at least noteworthy to see how many respondents shared the sentiment that the demarcation lines between the organizations involved in the delivery of public services became blurred under media pressure, and that media policy could be one of the explanatory factors for the loss of autonomy that a number of public organizations have recently experienced.

6.4 Substitution: the daily yardstick

The third and last aspect of mediatization is substitution: do mediated activities substitute for formerly non-mediated activities? Also on this level, there are many forms of mediatization in public organizations. The most tangible form of mediatization is the allocation of time: the office time non media people spend on the media. Respondents from government departments naturally report that they sometimes donate large portions of their time to media related work. But also some people from more or less autonomous organizations are sometimes called upon. The communications officer of a statutory authority providing politically salient services, for instance indicates that "when elections come, your workload and priorities change dramatically, because the government will try to win the elections and this could mean that we do different things, have different priorities."

Some executives spend considerable time on the media, although this varies greatly. The executive of a third sector organization with a large public profile for instance notes how (s)he uses about 30 minutes a day of office time "scanning key media reports and summaries". Another executive from an organization with a much smaller media profile however indicates to spend about fifteen to twenty per cent of the time on media. (S)he is always accessible to media and will often answer calls from journalists – even on Sundays – in person. And a third executive with a large media presence recalls:" I have an open door for the media. I spend about twenty-five percent of my time talking to the media; I answer calls myself and will just about always cooperate."

In some situations, executives note that they take the media effects of their choices into consideration when they make important policy decisions. A Dutch executive for instance referred to a specific and far reaching policy decision that was partly founded on the presumption that they did not dare the risk of a policy disaster and ensuing media storm. They wanted to avoid reputational damage in a situation with far-reaching implications for the benefactors of the public service. Another respondent notes how the reputational aspect is formally integrated in their decision making on interventions:

> "Dealing with reputation is a specific part of our decision trees. There are two types of risks. You could fail to see a problem so we are the last to know. Reputationally, that would be very damaging for us. So we have installed a whole apparatus not to miss the warning signs. The other risk is over-reacting, and that we forever turn up with the ambulance but that there is no incident. That would be very damaging for our reputation as well and overburdening (…). We are very alert to getting our judgment right."

When the media are part of decision making processes, this also affects policy preparations and policy outcomes. A respondent for instance recalls how in the restructuring of their social policy program:

> "From day one is how to get it through the media is on your mind. Because you know, if you don't curtail this, stories about sad people are going to be broadcast in the news all day. So you do many things that are not strictly necessary for your policies but that are necessary to get it through the media and to control a media fire storm."

A Dutch respondent describes a similar case, where a controversial policy proposal was deliberately developed in such a way that it would be acceptable in an age of critical media. In this specific case, the policy process was coordinated from day one with societal partners and related interest groups. Some respondents, particularly working for central government departments, looked at this development with dread. They stated: "We feel that the policy is becoming second to the media strategy", and: "Much policy is driven by media". The high value of "media responsiveness has given the media the room to drive the policy agenda." Many others, however, described the importance of the media in more neutral terms, claiming it was a critical constraint in change processes that however, when managed properly, could be turned into a potential enabler of success.

A final form of substitution is where success in the external media becomes a yardstick for measuring internal success. A Dutch respondent for instance notes how an executive with a good media performance brings confidence and a sense of control to public organizations. It also helps them with their cause or so the respondents feel. They experience that a good reputation is a phenomenal asset in their external relations and for instance helps third sector organizations in their competition for funds, where they feel that a "strong reputation puts you in a better position to win the fight for a limited pool of money." The same thing is noted for government departments, where some executives express that they believe that a positive media presence helps them in the annual fight over the budgets. Media success is also a yardstick for public approval and organizational legitimacy. A respondent notes how "people ask, why are we going to spend a hundred million on this or that if the public don't appreciate it and if the media will bag it?"

The daily yardstick also works for inter-collegial assessments: people working for organizations with a large and positive media presence see boosts in staff morale and in the behavior of people. A senior respondent observed how the media were used as a measure for internal relevance and seniority, (s)he said:

> "It is a daily yardstick – although not very accurate – that everybody uses to measure everybody else. You walk into a meeting and establish your credibility immediately by referring to a terrible article in this or that...' It is a sort of status instrument, if you meet a colleague after a terrible night with the media and (s)he doesn't even know about the issue, you think: 'It infuriates me that (s)he doesn't know'."

6.5 Mediatization of throughputs in sum

This chapter has described how organizational processes within public service providers – organizational throughputs – have become mediatized in a large number of ways. Some of the critical observers and respondents felt that the media agenda has become so dominant in policy processes that solid and genuine policy considerations have been more or less crowded out. And some other critical external observers referred to the sometimes abrasive methods used by communications officers to enforce message control (Barns 2005; Ester 2007) and the restrictive effects on advocacy of governmental work for third sector organizations (Maddison & Hamilton 2007).

The table below lists the different aspects of mediatization that have been discussed in the course of this chapter.

The levels of mediatization differ between different types of organizations. When we compare the different types of organizations, it is, as it was in earlier chapters, again obvious that central government departments experience a much higher level of mediatization than public and third sector service providers. The organizations closest to the ministers 'suffered' the most from mediatization, as a large portion of the news relates to their work and they are highly dependent on social actors (for instance principals and teachers) as well as politicians; both of which are more or less outside of their control. The large third sector service providers were conversely more professional in the accommodation of throughputs to media demands. They needed to follow up on the media to a much lesser extent, probably to a large degree due to the fact that they are less often the target of critical media stories. Third sector service providers are generally able, provided they operate in newsworthy areas, to set the agenda for their own media stories. And they do so to a large extent – as do public service providers – as will be elaborated in the next chapter.

Table 5: Overview mediatization organizational throughputs

Accommodation	Amalgamation	Substitution
• Communications departments (media minders; media units; PR; Whole-of-Government Coordination) • Centrality of communications departments • Occupational transformation: hiring people with media backgrounds • Codes for media conduct • Media training • Documentation and archiving (and FOI concerns) • Internal communication (and FOI concerns) • Reporting policies (timing and crowding) • Facilitator of organizational transformations	• Internal communication via external media • Media alertness • Permanent risk assessment • Early calls • Anticipation of queries • Checking and correcting factual information • Preparing swift responses • Backgrounding • Media-adapted policy advise • Intra-organizational centralization • Inter-organizational centralization • (Potential) tension media- and non-media people • Who is the messenger?	• Allocation of attention and office hours • Aspect of decision making • Affects decision outcomes • Yardstick for external success • Yardstick for internal success

7. Mediatization of Organizational Outputs

"Control function' and increased recognition of our organization."

"Education of community about services and expectation management."

"Supporting strategy and brand outcomes (goals)."

"Keep public informed / encourage open debate / independent scrutiny of outcomes policy."

Above are some of the first observations that participants in focus groups submitted to paper when asked to describe the most important function of the media for their organization. About a third of the respondents, some of them are quoted above, mentioned functions of the media that directly referred to the *outputs* of the organization, such as the delivery of services or general organizational strategy. Interestingly, as is noticeable in the quotations above, those respondents were for some reason or another unable to mention just *one* function of the media, even though they were asked to do so. These respondents generally felt inclined to collate a number of distinct but evidently indistinguishable roles the media played for them. This suggests that organizational exchanges with the media always have a complex and layered character: they serve (selfish) strategic aims for the person and the organization *and* (noble) causes of service delivery to the people. The media are instrumental tools that organizations may choose to utilize, and thus try to control, while they are simultaneously institutions of their own that defy outside control by service providers (or others). This multifaceted character of the media – at the same time associated with deeply selfish *and* highly noble behavior; a greatly used practical instrument that nevertheless always threatens to explode in your face – seems fundamental to understanding the role of the media in the provision of public services. Consider for instance the ambiguities in the response below, provided by a highly experienced Australian public service provider, who was answering the question why her organization chose to use the media quite aggressively:

"Also it seems to be important and legitimate. Some provisions of the (…) Act gives our organization the room to explain publicly what we are doing. Also there are a number of legitimate reasons for seeking publicity. One of them is the fact that Parliament has passed an important Act, people should (…) know their rights and obligations. Also it is a form of accountability to do what you're doing very publicly. Obviously it also builds support for our cause. It's a way of countering incorrect information, built up by people that we can redress."

This chapter will look at the mediatization of organizational outputs: the delivery of public services in an extra-organizational context. We will start out by examining how public organizations accommodate the (news) media in their outputs, in part by investigating the ways in which their organizational websites cater to journalistic demands. We will then proceed to discuss substitution (substitution of formerly non-mediatized outputs for mediatized outputs) and amalgamation (how non-media outputs become affected by mediatization).

7.1 A mediatized playing field

Public organizations were traditionally renowned for their secretive behavior. Public organizations and bureaucracies do not generally work in the spotlights of the media and they are traditionally considered to be sealed as oysters; keeping their valuables safely inside. This picture might have been true in the past – although it is certainly vastly exaggerated – but it is certainly no longer applicable in the current age. Blumler and Kavanagh (1999) have asserted that we are now living in the *third age of political communication*, where political and policy discussions to a large degree take place through the media. This third age is characterized by increased competitive pressures between media, a centrifugal diversification of media channels, anti-elitist popularization and populism, and an intensified professionalization of political communication. The rise of web 2.0 and the social media might, following this line of reasoning, perhaps already have given us the *fourth age* of political communication. Nevertheless, the observations concerning anti-elitism (and government), diversification, competition and professionalization, not only refer to the central actors in democracies, such as politicians, their parties and central governments, but they also hit the mark for service providers. Most large public service providers, be it from the public or from the third sector, are highly active in their media environments. The strategic environment of the delivery of public services has to some extent been transferred to the media arena.

The figure below describes how respondents assess the extent to which the behavior of their *counterparts* has become mediatized in the sense that the other – be it the service provider (public or third sector) or the advocacy organization – make active use of the media.

Figure 7: Mediatization of policy field

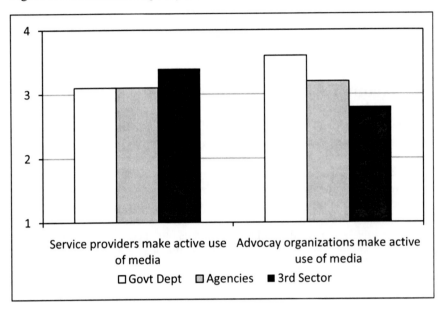

The figure above first of all suggests that most respondents feel that 'the other' uses the media to a larger extent than they do themselves. Advocacy organizations are expectedly seen as more heavy media users than service providers (although the line between these two types of organizations may have become blurred for many third sector organizations). And the further the respondent is removed from the other – e.g. government departments – the heavier the others' mediatization is conceived to be.

The focus groups confirmed this view of a relatively mediatized strategic playing field, where people would often feel that 'the other' was doing more media than they were doing themselves. The different parties, partners or contenders, in a policy field do some of their operations via the media, and media attention is also used as a viable threat. One Dutch respondent for instance describes how his counterparts will sometimes tell that they "aim to write a letter to Parliament, that will also be sent to the minister and to the newspapers, and they will ask how we feel about that. They're basically testing the water." And another respondent adds: "Causing a stir is just one of the tactics in negotiations". A third respondent compared these tactics to football, where a certain level of foul play is acceptable and players know that their opponents may bend and cross some of the formal rules. Breaches of the more subtle and socially negotiated informal rules, however, are not acceptable and will have repercussions. Participants in public service provision are thus allowed to use the media strategically, although they need to exert a great deal of good judgment in this regard to prevent their media strategies from backfiring or causing rifts with important partners.

7.2 Accommodation: in and out of the spotlights

Accommodation refers to the organizational structures and processes with which public service providers directly engage with the media; here on the level of organizational outputs, such as services but also external communications and strategic positioning. On this level, there is an important distinction between devising, planning and putting out one's own communication products and responding to the often unsolicited questions by journalists. The strategic aims in those instances are often the exact opposites: it is about creating maximal *or* minimal media exposure. We will start with the latter, because many respondents suggested that their ability to stay out of the spotlights is sometimes more critical than their capacity to get into the spotlights.

Staying out of the spotlights

Minimal exposure, or even annulment of a potential article, is very often the aim of an organization when journalists call and start digging into an issue. "It is our goal to get off the front pages", one respondent from a heavily criticized service provider stated, and many others spoke in a similar vein. Others for instance noted "For us the test is: does a story go away quickly. If it goes away fast, that is a success", and: "Not getting them in the media is important, it's a lot of what we do", and: "A successful day can be a story not running." Staying out of the media's focus, preventing stories from running, or minimizing the effects or the duration of the stories that couldn't be prevented, are all important aspects of media management. A respondent from a third sector organization delivering public services provided a telling example that is quoted at length below:

> "Sometimes it takes our media guy more time to bury something than it does to bring a story out. We do that a lot. An example? Well, actually this example *did* hit the papers but it was not big TV news. It was a pedophile story (…). He was kicked out of a home, there's a huge outcry, almost public lynching. We got a call and we put him somewhere. We cannot judge. He's been there for two months. Two days from him going to the next place, the story broke. The story was that we were giving shelter to (…). What could have been quite ugly, was the part of giving shelter to this type with public money. But it worked out well, it kind of blew over. Our media guy spent an hour speaking to one of the broadcasting guys to bring it down about running a story in the mainstream news about it. He was basically appealing to the moral sense of the

journalist. What was to be gained by running a story on this guy, a posse of media people camping outside the home, causing distress for all the clients? So we put the broadcasting people in a spin for several hours until they came back and said: 'We have been discussing morals for the last several hours and have decided not to run it.' Well, miracles happen!"

The reasons public service providers try to limit the level of news making on a topic is generally because they feel that the spin or the perspective on the story is unbalanced or even harmful to the service, their organization's reputation or their clients. "What are we to gain by bringing these people in front of the camera'?", one respondent for instance notes, as they "aren't going to be photogenic, and the journalists are going to dig as deep in the holes as possible".

A number of *techniques* are used to keep unwelcome stories away from the spotlights of the news and to decrease the impact of those stories once their appearance can't be prevented. Very often it takes extra information from the service provider to make sure that stories don't run. "Sometimes we give them so much information", a respondent for instance notes, "and make it so comprehensive, that it will not run". Some services are very complicated and do not translate well into the simple stories the media need to broadcast and write, so "we try to explain the policy, language, structures… that can help cut out some of the non-productive stories you sometimes have". "Another strategy" another respondent notes, "is to downplay it. Often, media reports are grossly exaggerated." In talking to the journalist, extreme care is taken in using the proper wordings and to avoid alerting the journalist to follow-up news. Journalists often like to extrapolate from single incidents – for instance on a school – to larger social issues that "will spark at least one and a half hour of talkback radio" – for instance on the education system or the perils of contemporary parenting. In response, the public service provider will do as best as (s)he can to bring the issue back to the specific incident. "Usually", a respondent states, "the best way is being careful in providing details, not holding something back, but be careful how you explain. And just ensure that there's nothing more to find. Then it usually goes away".

All in all, it takes considerable media contact from the organizational spokespeople to prevent unwelcome publications from running. Being able to do that presupposes productive and trusted media relations and an open line with journalists. The executive of a very media-cautious organization, for instance, that nurtures the attitude that "the media are there to be observed and not participate in", nevertheless indicates that they will cooperate with media on stories that will run anyway, even when they are negative. The reason is that they want to make sure that at least the facts are correct. In addition, it ensures them that there is a line of communication between the journalist and the service provider. The relationship with the journalist is an important asset in these issues, many respondents note, as it will help them to prevent some of the "borderline-stories", a spokesperson says, although it will never prevent journalists from running the "big stories." After all, journalists are always on duty, even when they speak of the record, as the Dutch ministry of defense wants its employees to be aware of (Boom 2010).

There is, finally, no set rule with which to respond to potentially critical and harmful media inquiries; it always takes a lot of situational judgment. A media-respondent states: "You always make a decision on an allegation: deny, not commenting, being proactive and putting someone up... If it's a denial, we have to be *absolutely* certain." And another respondent added:

> "Sometimes not doing an interview is a possibility to keep it from running. If it is likely to be an ongoing issue, you better keep out. Because conversely, if you go on and give them a talking head, you actually give them a story they might not have had otherwise."

The *type of response* offered, thus, also matters. A strategically wise response can be helpful to abbreviate the length of a media episode. One respondent for instance notes how they will always refrain from comments in individual issues but rather focus on the aggregate level or the structure of the service or policy in general. And sometimes, specifically live on radio or television, spokespersons will deliberately return to the same point, irrespective of the question. This will make the interviewer change the subject, because it will obviously annoy the viewers and listeners. Often curt and factual answers can be helpful. Consider for instance the statement underneath, from a self-expressed "gun-shy" organization:

> "We only comment on erroneous media interests. Last time was a comment by a politician, it had the potential to be misleading, saying we did something that we hadn't. It got a particular spin on it. So we gave a reaction, to stop the potential spin coming out of it. So: *these* are the facts, *this* is what we have done. Just the facts, *bang, bang, bang*! End of statement. No debate, no follow up, no press conference. Just the facts."

Whatever the response is, it is always critical to respond *quickly*. Many large organizations have critical incident teams, which are informed as soon as a critical question or issue pops up anywhere around the organization. These critical incident teams sometimes even respond proactively before anything 'happens' in the news. If there is an ugly incident within or in association with the organization, for instance, it is important to respond via the radio and also the net. "The availability and readiness to go on is how your whole organization is judged. Essentially it is important symbolic action that shows you are a public service that listens to complaints." A quick response is important as "conventional wisdoms are hard to challenge". In order to do so, criticized organizations feel they need to "constantly engage with the debate and provide data to bat away the allegations". And: "If you don't manage the negative ones, they [citizens and journalists, TS] will not believe the positive ones."

In all of the instances above, public service providers were actively trying to minimize the level of attention in the news for issues journalists were pursuing. In many other instances, however, public service providers will actively contact all sorts of media in order to create a maximum exposure for their messages. In doing so, public organizations will often, consciously or not, exploit the media logic of the institution. We will look at this in more detail in chapter 8; for now we will first look at the general strategy in using media as an output in itself.

Newman and Perloff (2004) have described how the media strategies of current political actors, such as presidents, are largely similar to the more general marketing techniques that are customary in the private sector. Their claim is that winning the white house is not dissimilar from making a profit or selling a specific product. The similarity lies in the nature of the activities involved. Marketing and campaigning both rest on a combination of research, targeting audiences, strategic positioning and communication products that aim to win over voters or consumers in a competitive environment. The same observation can be made about the communications strategies of public service providers: they often engage in the same activities and will also use communicative tools – working with journalists or around journalists – in order to develop their 'market'.

The respondents from third sector organizations were the only ones in this research project who actively used the word 'marketing' to describe their publicity work. Third sector organizations also seemed to be more eager to recruit experienced marketers from business sectors, or at least spoke about it more freely than public sector respondents do. This does not necessarily mean that their practices differ to a great extent, but rather suggests that the aims and backgrounds may vary between different sectors. Particularly, third sector organizations were willing to speak about it more openly in strategic terms. One respondent from a third sector organization that uses media with a great deal of success for instance described the process as follows:

> "Bringing out a magazine gave us the opportunity to speak with publishers about advertising. They know how to do it and we had the opportunity to learn from them. We have then learnt how to translate this to cause-related marketing. It was a blue ocean strategy, really a completely new way of thinking, which turned out to have many advantageous spin offs. (...) I wouldn't be so arrogant to say that we thought all these spin offs were going to happen, it was a real learning curve for us. And it was very obvious very quickly that this was a good way of gaining revenue".

To a large extent, choosing and 'exploiting' the proper communication channel is the key strategic decision to be made. *Channeling* has become an ever bigger issue in the context that Blumler and Kavanagh (1999) described as 'centrifugal diversification of media channels'. In times of crisis, dealing with the massive character of news interests from pack journalism, is a real issue for public organizations, which also propels the civil service and some service providers into the spotlights of the media. Politicians can't possibly deal with all the media requests. Some senior civil servants express that they feel they have to do some of the share of the media work, as there is just so much media that the minister can't possibly do it her- or himself. And a communications officer adds: "I just need everybody to *shut up*, in order to be able to deal with all issues, one at a time".

A very first decision is: which medium do we use? In a centrifugal media environment, service providers will more often shun the general and inclusive press coverage via press conferences and mainstream media and will much rather seek out the medium that they expect to serve their cause most strategically (see Ester 2007: 117). The reasons and focus differs greatly between organizations. "For us", one third sector organization states, "the focus will be on business media, for instance in the waiting rooms of airports." Other respondents prefer talkback radio, "as the news spreads from there", or "soft news, that allow you to say what you want", or the local press "that likes our good news stories", or even "Chinese or middle east media". Very often, it is not about prioritizing one specific medium but about creating a specific mix of channels. "We sometimes use mainstream media and will sometimes use specialist media. It is important for us to be published and have things there as well." The new digital media are often an extension to the existing media package: "We work multi-channel, multi-sensory."

Respondents are well aware of how the different media have their pros and cons. The good thing, from the perspective of organizations, about new media and coproduced magazines of course is that they "cut out the middle man" – the journalist – and allow organizations to publish their materials undistorted by interpretations. Very often, however, they still need the old media, although decreasingly so, to reach a larger public, particularly in policy circles. The press gallery in Parliament: "Has a very narrow range and asks very predictable questions. They always look for the frame of political contest". The newspapers provide appreciated context and often allow interviewees to see and correct the stories before they appear. However, the editorial process may produce a header that puts the whole story in a different perspective. In comparison, "on the radio, the chance of misquoting is much less", as a respondent notes, but, as another adds "you run the risk of getting questions that weren't discussed before, and you must be prepared to give a reasonably honest answer." Where most organizations deliberately seek out the most advantageous pack of news reporting, some highly media sensitive organizations rather rely on the 'traditional', inclusive press conference for a large public. For some of them it is a matter of principle: "We either speak to everybody and ensure that everybody has an equal chance to hear this, or we don't make a comment". This policy sometimes also has a strategic undercurrent:

"The journalist may misunderstand, so when we only speak to one of them, there are no safeguards. A media conference can be safer than speaking to just one person. About a quarter of the journalists will get it wrong in one way while another quarter will get it wrong the other way. It's a safeguard, they will even out."

One of the safest and most practical ways of ascertaining the desired content and to keep message control, is to cooperate with media and to coproduce content. One respondent for instance describes how they sometimes want to bring specific issues to the public's attention and on the public agenda. They will then ask a specialized medium to cover it and will provide them with the necessary data, facts and respondents. Others explain that they sometimes coproduce events with media, which gives them a big chance of coverage, providing the media find the issue newsworthy.

Another route is to focus on non-journalistic media, such as websites, TV-shows, airline magazines, events, community shows, advertorials, sponsoring of popular sports outfits, etc. Well-known – even broadcasted in Europe – are the Australian shows Border security and Bondi Rescue. In the Netherlands and Belgium there is a popular police series, partially financed by a municipality and the police. Exciting as these forms may be, most use of non-journalistic media is in the form of magazines, as people "have an insatiable appetite for magazines". In these co-productions with media, organizations ascertain that all the facts are correct and they aspire to reach their target audiences. In order to do so, they must make sure that they provide interesting and instructive stories and refrain from the traditional preoccupation with "flashing logos". It is the message that is important, and if the message comes across well this may reap all sorts of benefits for the organization that is associated with the message.

All in all, organizations make many decisions with which they accommodate the outside media reality, either by staying away from potentially harmful coverage or by initiating and exploiting specific forms of coverage. In both instances, they strive to keep control of their messages and try to defend or bolster their reputations. There is a thin line here between marketing the organization and genuine communication to the public, where organizations use a wide array of communicative instruments in addition to the 'traditional', inclusive press moments. A very specific and relatively new instrument is the organizational website, which we will explore below in some more depth, as this helps to illustrate just how organizations create outputs that are geared to the news media.

7.3 Mediatization of organizational websites

Organizational websites are a specific media-tool that organizations can use to get into the spotlights of the news media. Websites are a medium themselves, of course, but they are also used as triggers for coverage by news media and as aides for journalists working on a story. But the website, and other types of internal media or social media, are also used as alternative channels to the general news media with which organizations send messages without the inevitable 'distortion' by journalists. Simultaneously, however, websites also provide information that is specifically designed for the news media and is supposed to be helpful in attracting (or evading) interested journalists. The websites of 56 Australian and Dutch public and third sector service providers have been analyzed with this last question in mind: the extent to which they cater to the needs of journalists.

Why would websites be relevant to journalists in the first place, one may wonder? The advent of the internet has dramatically changed the work of journalists over the last fifteen years. The internet of course harbors immeasurable quantities of free information, albeit without properly discriminating between fact and fad. As journalists need to have swift access to information, their daily routines have changed. Journalists now spend more and more time behind desks, checking and searching for online information, instead of roaming the corridors of power for loose-lipped sources or misplaced official documents (see Deuze 2002). Finding information is no longer a problem; finding *reliable* information, however, can be more critical or even problematic. It is here that organizational websites may come in handy. They are accessible beyond normal office hours, may contain the official data that journalists need to substantiate their stories and also present organizations with a simple platform where they can present themselves and their positions on crucial issues.

Websites provide information for different audiences and it is, from the outset, not always clear which audience is targeted by a website. Also, the information and visuals on display can be meant to be informative to a variety of audiences. And some (parts of) websites are undoubtedly designed *without* any designated audience; they are simply based on routine, copied from elsewhere or inherited from the set format of the company that built the website. Nevertheless, a content analysis of organizational websites, analyzing both elements of contents as well as the accessibility of that content, can bare the extent to which they are geared towards the needs of journalists. Overall, four types of journalistic needs may be satisfied by an organization's website: swift access to reliable information, early warning of newsworthy events, access to spokespersons, and additional data with which they can add the human face to stories. We will discuss below how the websites of Dutch and Australian service providers are catering to those journalistic needs.

The very first feature of journalistic work is that journalists often need reliable information on policies or organizations with which they may not be familiar a half day before they write or broadcast about them. They thus need to have *swift access to reliable information* on many issues of public policy. The websites of public service providers are used as platforms where reliable information for journalists (and many others) is displayed. As table 6 below suggests, organizational websites cater – consciously or not – to this journalistic need by their sheer existence in the first place, but also because they will generally offer free access to corporate information, publish corporate and policy information, offer podcasts and videos, and, not in the last place, offer a concise 'facts and figures' section. This last section in particular can be very useful for journalists. Almost half of (the larger) service providers use their websites to present key indicators about for instance their revenues, numbers of employees, numbers and types of clients and sometimes the honors they have won ('most innovative public organization', for instance). These data are often used and republished in news stories.

In journalistic selection routines, the highly ambiguous criterion of newsworthiness – generally defined as 'important' and 'interesting' news (Cook 2005: 5) – is of crucial importance. An essential aspect of the news is that it must contain something 'new'. Also, the news should be brought to the attention of the journalists, who are the gatekeepers to the news. Organizations do this all the time; journalists are incessantly contacted by people and organizations competing for entrance to the news with a stream of *information subsidies*. Organizational websites are, modest but not unimportant, tools with which public service providers try to inform journalists (and others) about their news. Table 6 shows that organizations are using a variety of means to this end which – again: consciously or not– cater for this journalistic need. Their websites will generally contain a designated 'News section', will display their news and press releases, will single out upcoming events, and websites often pile up their newsletters. None of these information subsidies are likely to have huge impacts on the news, organizations will nevertheless use them as minor cogs in their larger news-making (and news-avoiding) strategies. In addition, the evolving innovations in web technology has brought forward mechanisms with which journalists (and others) may be alerted to an organization's news, such as tag clouds (that depict search words with a high saliency), rss-feeds, and, of course, organizational twitter- and social media pages.

Once a journalist has become interested in an organization for his or her story, a further need is often *access to a spokesperson*. Journalists often need to ask for more information, may want to check story lines and facts, and may ask for a formal response from the organization or someone "to go on" on television or the radio. Organizational websites can cater to this need by providing direct contact details to a spokesperson or by displaying the section 'media center' (or something similar). As table 6 suggests, 40 to 70% of Australian and Dutch service providers were found to provide the media with an easy access to spokespersons.

Furthermore, should journalists wish to proceed and to make a full story on the organization and its services, they will often want to personalize the story and to cast it with a human face. This can be a challenging task, particularly for large public service providers who (sometimes) by definition need to operate with a certain degree of bureaucratic anonymity. Nevertheless, some service providers have dared to stray away from traditional anonymity and have pursued their public images in a more personalized style (Mulgan 2002; Schillemans & Van Thiel 2009). Their websites are to some extent used as tools that may enable journalists to add personal touches to stories about otherwise fairly abstract organizations flying under the banners of unutterable abbreviations ("the 'ACCC' now issues ..."). Most service providers ascertain that their director or chief executive officer is easily found and only two or three mouse clicks away. And about two thirds of the agencies will also provide flattering pictures and personal profiles or CVs. In addition, some of the highly newsworthy service providers offer high quality photographs that can be used directly by journalists in their publications. With these measures, service providers assist journalists who need to crank out a story in the final instance.

In the table below, the different ways in which websites cater to the needs of journalists are listed and the relative prevalence of all of these forms on the websites of the investigated service providers – public and third sector – is displayed.

Table 6: Overview mediatization organizational websites

Journalistic need	Item	Public service providers	Third sector organizations
Swift access to reliable information	Organizational website as such	98%	100%
	Corporate information	100%	100%
	Corporate documentation / reports	97%	100%
	Non-corporate documentation / reports	85%	89%
	Podcasts / video's	35%	33%
	Facts & figures section	40%	67%
News alerts	News section	90%	89%
	Press releases (in average annual nrs)	77	65
	Events	63%	89%
	Newsletter	69%	78%
	Rss-button	59%	33%
	Social media link	4%	67%
	Tag cloud	4%	22%
Access to spokespersons	'Mediacenter '	40%	67%
	Direct link to media spokesperson	70%	44%
Personalized stories	CEO easily found (in average nr of mouse clicks)	2,7	2,0
	Personal information on CEO	65%	67%
	Website provides a photo of the CEO	60%	78%
	Downloadable, publishable photos	26%	22%

The table above, again, suggests that organizational websites do indeed cater to the needs of journalists. The table also suggests, for the first time in this book, that third sector organizations overall make more use of media than their counterparts from the public sector. In important ways, their websites were more advanced than those of the public service providers. The websites of third sector service providers for instance offer more 'facts & figures sections', do more often contain media centers, events sections and they also make a lot more use of social media and newer technologies such as twitter, Facebook and tag clouds. These findings make sense when we take into account that third sector organizations are more directly dependent on active support from citizens. This makes it more important to use all available means of communication. Also, many third sector organizations complain about lacking media interests (see Maddison & Hamilton 2007); another reason for them perhaps to push a little harder to get their stories into the news.

7.4 Substitution & amalgamation: government by publicity

Organizational websites are but one from a wide variety of methods used by public service providers to attain media coverage. Media attention can be important for a number of reasons. According to McKay and Paletz (2004: 323), policy actors will often seek publicity in order to rally public opinion on their side, to pressurize Parliament or bureaucracies, to place items on the agendas of others, to build prestige, persuade people to put pressure on other policy makers or to promote specific measures. 'Doing' media has been branded as 'government by publicity', where words are more and more the real actions of policy actors (Cook 2005: 124; see also Kepplinger 2002). The media work may come as an addition to the organization's core business, but publicity also serves the organization's goals and is incorporated into either existing organizational strategies (amalgamation) or can even substitute for those.

The most visible form of *amalgamation* occurs when the overall media strategy of an organization becomes interwoven with, or even plays a central role in, its overarching general strategy. Earlier we saw that a number of senior level respondents felt that the substance of policies was sometimes threatened to become second to the prime goal of communication. A number of CEOs pointed in the same direction during the interviews. They would not directly concede that delivering policies now comes second to communication, of course. However, they *did* claim that communication was now at the heart of their organization's strategy, particularly in times of organizational transformation. One director from a large third sector organization for instance describes how they are pursuing a "new strategy, with growth and more centralization. Communication and marketing are one of the three areas where more investments need to be made." Others spoke in the same vein, claiming they were "instilled with the deliberate task of raising the organization's profile", that "a high media profile is a deliberate strategic choice", or that "sponsors want the organization to have a public profile".

Strategic choices can be affected by media considerations. A CEO for instance stated that: "We targeted some issues at the start that would spark public interest." This doesn't mean that decisions are exclusively driven by publicity considerations, the respondents would (probably) strongly disagree with that conclusion, but the media are often essential to strategic plans and innovations and they are often ever-present in the backs of their mind in routine decision making. As a former CEO of a large public service provider describes:

> "When we set up the current organization, there was just so much to do, the media were very small in my mind. We were out there getting contracts, doing something that had never been

done before. Integrating IT systems, dealing with (…), everybody looking over our shoulder. The media were not dominant, but nevertheless, they were present in every step we took and we appointed a board member who dealt exclusively with the media".

Governing by publicity can serve a number of causes. To begin with, the media can become part (amalgamation) or even the sole tool (substitution) of *service delivery*. Particularly organizations whose services depend on and interact with the attitudes, behaviors and choices of its recipients, service providers in health care, safety of all sorts, and education, sometimes use a lot of targeted media in delivering their services. Specific campaigns are for instance set up to fight drowning in the summer season, eating and food issues around Christmas, and sometimes organizations go public in response to critical incidents in order to stress the importance of their issue. Alford (2009) has argued that clients of public services are very often also *co-producers* in the delivery of the desired social outcomes of a service. One's health may for instance be partially dependent on the actions of the health care system, but in the 'production' of individual health, one's own lifestyle and consumption patterns are of course highly critical. Many public services rely on these types of coproduction with their clients; many public organizations accordingly use media as an enabler that persuades citizens to 'co-produce'. One respondent for instance declared: "We want to engage people in the community, so we need to engage with people to care about their environment. They must understand our programs, know that there's a reason for doing this, and understand that they could play a major role".

For service providers with regulatory tasks, the internet can be used as a forceful way of 'naming and shaming' that helps compliance and generally contributes to accomplishing their policy outcomes (see Pawson 2002). A name and shame website is in itself already a medium for messages, but very often the news media will pick up on the outcomes and write stories on the organizations at the bottom or the top of the list. And it sometimes is cost-efficient to use the media as a way of enhancing adherence to the law (Cook 2005:148). Handling the media in this respect requires a lot of tact and judgment: the act or statute of the organization should contain the possibility to do so, one should weigh ones words with utmost care and understand that it may invoke "*massive* adverse publicity with a very powerful effect." It is always important to be fair and precise in one's wording and not cross over the line and engage in "trial by media" (Yeung 2005).

Media publications can also serve as *investigative tools*. For the police, for instance, the media can be a very effective investigation tool, as they may "have a dead body, and don't know who did it". The release of information by the police usually sparks of a lot of activities by people and always produces a lot of information. Media publications may also spark off discussions and activities on the internet that in their turn can be informative for service providers. One Dutch

117

organization for instance claimed to have hired "cyber cops that search the net for some activities and certain products".

These first forms of substitution and amalgamation all pertained to the execution of the *task* of a public service provider. The next set of forms is focused more clearly on the *strategic positioning* of the organization as a prerequisite to its task.

In a general sense, public organizations incorporate or rely on the media to *address* their various *stakeholders*. Clients are the most notable stakeholders to be contacted. A survey on Dutch service providers elucidated how most service providers will (also) use local or sometimes national media as a method to contact their clients (Brandsen et al 2010). The *detour* via the media can be helpful, as "the community will only hear from us via the media". For third sector organizations who work on donations, this is obviously important, as "fifty per cent of the people register because of TV coverage". The media can also be helpful to contact the executives of related institutions who may respond more strongly to media coverage than to direct mail. And the media are important to reach the centers of power in Canberra, The Hague, London and other capitals. The quote below summarizes quite well how public service providers use the media, and in passing the quote also refers to the ongoing importance of the 'old' media for public services. The CEO of a public agency stated: "I want to target the people who read the quality papers … It's a way of getting towards MP's" (Deacon & Monk 2001a: 37).

There can be many reasons to contact the power centers through the media. The media can be used to put issues on the *agenda* or to raise their position on agendas. Organizations will try to "influence the image formation on dossiers" and "expose existing policy debates through the press". Several respondents also indicated how they used publicity to further specific policy issues. And another respondent stated how s(he) tried to ensure that "if politicians read in the press everyday what we're doing, they will distance themselves a bit from what they're told by (…)." Agenda setting loosely spills over into *lobbying*, something some organizations may do via the media, whereas some others stick to more covert forms of lobbying. Some organizations will also use news media for *advocacy*. Particularly third sector organizations indicated that they used media to this end, although they acceded that this could be a precarious strategy. It requires a lot of judgment. Finally, coverage in the news media may help organizations to *acquire new tasks, larger budgets* or *new assignments*. A respondent from a third sector organization for instance notes: "Media coverage can drive ministers to ask us if we can do something about an issue".

All in all, media attention is always a move in contested policy arenas that can be helpful to one's cause (if judged well) or catapult back on organizations (when misjudged). An executive, who describes the media as something he "holds in high concern as an instrument of power", explains his or her thoughts about the issue at some length below.

"Another reason (for using media, ts) was that I wanted to change the balance a bit. As I saw it, there was a kind of political equilibrium when I started, on a low level. The organization wasn't doing much when I started … and wasn't very effective. And that exactly matched the desires of the government in response to pressure from … I thought this was very undesirable … and what was needed was to step up the role of our organization. I could see this would cause political disequilibrium in the political environment. So we had to do something about that. So I thought there were a couple of important things to do. One was to be very public and engage with public opinion, media opinion etcetera and ultimately with political opinion. The other thing was to a degree at least to educate some of the other interest groups as to their true interests."

A final, important and probably rather obvious reason to use or integrate the news media in one's strategy, is to bolster your *reputation*. Reputation is an asset that will pay of dividends for all of the above mentioned goals. In the survey, all respondents agreed that it was crucial to avoid reputational damage through media stories. The highest score came from the third sector organizations (3,8) who seem to be most dependent on their reputation for support and resources. The other respondents answered slightly lower, between 3,3 and 3,5. The organizations thus feel that their reputation is important, a CEO from a public service provider explains, because "It's about money, getting the message across, have people participate; support voters as well, to influence politicians." A public service provider also links the reputation to funding:

"Why is reputation important? Funding could otherwise be difficult. Being a cause of stress for the minister may imply that you lose funding or functions or that you will be dissolved. A good reputation is necessary in order to function. This is not about the community, it is about politicians really. It is about the political environment in which we work, and the CEO know this full well and doesn't want that to happen."

7.5 Mediatization of outputs in sum

This chapter has described and discussed the mediatization of organizational outputs of public service providers, operating in more or less mediatized strategic policy fields. The chapter has clarified how, from the perspective of a public service provider, engaging with the media is perhaps almost as much about staying out of the news as it is about getting into the news. In both instances, organizations strive to control the messages that are circulated about themselves and their policies. Public service providers devote considerable resources to the tedious and complicated task of prohibiting (within their capacities) negative news stories from running. Simultaneously, of course, these organizations are also trying to spark off positive news stories.

Media strategies may be incorporated in the actual provision of public services and may also be integral to an organization's more general strategic public relations. Particularly organizations that are dependent on their environment to 'coproduce' in delivering services, do often resort to mediatized tactics. Positive news stories are thought to be helpful in persuading citizens to participate. On the strategic level, the media are an important channel for 'government by publicity', where the act of speaking is the actual output in a strategic policy field. Government by publicity can sometimes be beneficial, although it always requires accurate judgment, as it is difficult to control just how media stories evolve and the responses by relevant policy actors are not always predictable.

The table below summarizes the arguments on the mediatization of organizational outputs that have been developed in this chapter.

Table 7: Overview mediatization organizational outputs

Accommodation	Amalgamation & Substitution

• "Marketing":
   o Research
   o Targeting audiences
   o Strategic positioning
   o Developing communication products, such as websites
 	
 • Aim of media aides:
   o Provide reliable data
   o Provide news alerts
   o Access to spokespersons and responses
   o Personalization of stories
 	
 • Channeling of releases
 • Timing of releases
 • Strategic wording
 	
 • Develop relationships with media
 • Quick fired responses
 • Cooperation with media in production stories
	Media as tool in service delivery
	 • Naming & shaming
	 • Investigative tool
	 • Address stakeholders
	 • Persuade co producers
	
	 Media as part of public relations in general
	 • Agenda setting
	 • Lobbying
	 • Advocacy
	 • Acquisition (of tasks, budgets or assignments)
	 • Reputation management

This chapter has suggested that third sector service providers in some ways seem to be more mediatized than their cousins in the public sector. Testimony to this assertion comes from the comparison of organizational websites that showed how large third sector organizations have more advanced websites that are geared more to the needs of the average journalist. Also, respondents from third sector organizations would speak more liberally about their media and marketing strategies and their organizations would more commonly hire renown marketers from the profit sector. This suggests that the organizations who fare most literally on public support – third sector organizations – do most to present a good public image of themselves through the news media and other available media.

A second observation, already implicit above, is that organizations that depend on their clients to coproduce in bringing about the ultimate outcomes, will often use more elaborate media strategies than the other organizations. It is again a rational observation that suggests that the media can sometimes be a tool for service delivery, as it may summon essential stakeholders to take action.

This chapter on the mediatization of organizational outputs has developed into a rather instrumental discussion of how and when a public service provider can effectively 'use' the media. This specific angle has been inevitable, as a discussion with senior level respondents on how they use media strategies in order to attain their organizational goals, tends to become quite practical and instrumental. Nevertheless, the instrumentality of the chapter could falsely convey the impression that the news media are somehow a passive tool, awaiting utilization by service providers (and others). The chapter's focus could also falsely suggest that 'using media' is a genuinely *practical* issue, devoid of normative issues and considerations. The next two chapters are devised to correct these potential misreadings and will assess both the practical as well as the normative restrictions of 'government by publicity' by public service providers.

8. Media logic and public services

"Members of institutions recognize the potential of media logic vis-à-vis their goals of reaching an audience. In short, they present their own messages and images within the respectability and familiarity of media formats." (Altheide & Snow 1979: 244)

The argument in this book so far can be summarized in just one sentence: public services are provided by public and third sector organizations that have all, to varying degrees, become mediatized. The preceding chapters have endeavored to describe and analyze the various forms of organizational mediatization and, thus, sketched a picture of public organizations operating in demanding media environments. Whether any of this is of further interest depends on the answer to the follow up question: does mediatization *matter* (Livingstone 2009: 10). The main reason that so many researchers are studying the mediatization of politics and policy processes is that they work from the suspicion that media pressure invokes consequential institutional change. The underlying assumption is that institutions are colonized by the logic of the media and, accordingly, lose perspective on their traditional goals and functions. Media pressure is supposed to lead to organizational adaptation to media logic and, simultaneously, to the loss of core functions, goals and perspectives.

The concept of media logic was originally introduced by Altheide and Snow in 1979. The authors indicated that the media operate on the basis of their own institutional logic. This logic prescribes what types of subjects are important enough to discuss, what issues are relevant to the community and describes how the media become guardians of official and unofficial information (Altheide & Snow 1979: 237). They concluded that the institutional logic of the media permeated other social institutions. As they noted: "We find that rules for defining public events today are predominantly media rules – that is rules of strategy embedded in specific media formats." (1979: 246). Organizations that aim to contribute to public debates are more or less forced to respond to the media logic, which consists of a distinct set of aims, rules, production logics and constraints.

The concept of media logic serves very well to analyze how public service providers are able to use the media to their advantage, but also to illustrate some of the barriers they encounter and the risks involved.

8.1 Aims: making important news interesting

The most central aim of the media is to 'publish all the stories fit to print'. Newsworthiness is the central, although highly contingent and ambiguous, selection criterion that journalists use to sift through the immeasurable number of daily events in order to arrive at the limited number of stories which are, apparently, fit to print. This means, again speaking very generally, that journalists are looking for stories that are important as well as interesting (Cook 2005).

Public service providers have access to a lot of data and information that is of undisputed importance to the public. Especially the larger public service providers are the owners and producers of data on highly salient issues such as immigration, employment, crime, health and education. All the news these service providers want to bring across is naturally important from a public policy and public interest perspective. The problematic question for public service providers, however, is whether they are able to transform their important data and events into stories that are found interesting by journalists (and their audiences).

The interesting-criterion is problematic for most of the public service providers as they face difficulties in coming to terms with the set media rules for what is considered to be interesting. Interesting news often centers on renowned media personalities, most notably individuals, who bring the news. Many of the service providers are themselves not considered to be newsworthy. Particularly large public service providers are easily considered to be faceless and dense bureaucracies that are difficult to report on. They 'hide' behind abstract acronyms – the Dutch public sector for instance features the following important agencies: CPB, CBP, CBS, CBG, CVZ, CFV, and COA – and their spokespersons will often pose maximally neutral, in order to avoid the type of personalization that is important on TV. The same has been noted about third sector organizations that may experience a genuine disinterest by journalists (Maddison & Hamilton 2007).

The average news story will also focus on the exceptional case where something goes blazingly wrong or, conversely, is an amazing and unprecedented success. Public service providers, however, generally prefer to talk about overall patterns and developments in service provision. They are also prone to understand incidents as, however deplorable or tragic sometimes, just temporary and uncommon incidents in otherwise stable systems of service provision that work fine on balance. And they will know that only the fewest spectacular success stories are likely to survive as successes when examined carefully and in the longer run. Furthermore, public service providers also face restrictions in talking about individual cases of success or failure for legal reasons or just out of loyalty to their cooperative partners.

Finally, the average news story is likely to focus on political combat and discord, where one person's or party's position is challenged and opposed by another's, and both parties are prepared to stage their fight in front of the public. Public service providers are not the Weberian, neutral executioners of political decisions. They use a variety of techniques with which to influence decision making. However, these techniques will generally only be effective when deployed covertly. Public organizations have little to win from open conflicts and will try to discuss policy issues in abstract terms, with a focus on substance, and they will be careful to avoid confrontation with politicians, political parties or interest organizations.

In order to tackle the issue of 'interesting news', public service providers thus look for ways to bring their important news in interesting ways. A CEO from a large and successful third sector organization for instance put it as follows: "You always look for an unexpected angle, that doesn't really fit the box." The next sections will discuss some of the advantages service providers may have that may allow them to be considered interesting.

Apart from importance and interest, making a profit (or at least ascertaining their news organization's financial stability) is a naturally important organizational aim for the media. This fuels the competition between media for specific types of stories which, in turn, generally lends itself to exploitation by public service providers (and others who wish to enter the news). Public service providers will sometimes feed information to different media who may be eager to have the first scoop or may want to run specific types of stories as they are particularly profitable. An experienced communications officer for instance explained how it makes a big difference whether you operate in a one- or in a two-paper city, as your "bargaining position is much better" in the second situation. Competition between media is an asset for public organizations in their perpetual 'negotiation of newsworthiness' with journalists that allows them more control on the content of stories as they can use 'exit' towards the competitor as a viable 'threat'. Particularly the local media can be 'used' quite readily by public service providers as some of them have access to the types of stories that small-staffed local media are craving for: "good, local stories". A respondent for instance notes:

"Loads of local media want their local people in there. They really don't want a picture of the minister; they want their local principal, or raider or whatever. Also because they will sell more papers when Uncle Jeffrey is in the paper."

The competitive nature of the profit-making media is however not only a factor that can be exploited strategically; it is also a contingency that comes with some costs for public organizations seeking favorable coverage. One of the costs is for instance that the media will not only compete *for* stories, but do also compete each other *with* their stories, and will subsequently seek maximum exposure and controversy with the story. This means, for instance, as a Dutch respondent from a public service provider suggests, that policy actors are more or less forced to phrase their messages ever more forceful, in order to attain the desired effect. The risk of this strategy of course is that policy actors will choose wordings that are too stark or will create otherwise avoidable problems or ripples in their policy fields. In addition, some media will sensationalize stories in a way that runs counter to what participants understand as proper policy. An experienced respondent describes:

> "We wouldn't go to the tabloids with an issue. You avoid them like a plague because you can't trust them. They're there to sell a newspaper, and if they are able to link an outraging quote to us, they have a good story. So it is better not to give them the opportunity at all and we don't speak to them."

The competition between media is finally a potential hindrance to those, particularly third sector organizations, that coproduce productions with the media. The CEO of a media-savvy third sector organization for instance notes how they are involved with a strategic media-partner that "dislikes" their large, local newspaper. The media-partner always "wants the first bite of a story" so they can't "give" it to the local newspaper, but sometimes "they won't run it big enough and that's a real barrier."

The pattern here is similar to the patterns we will see below: media logic is sometimes useful for public service providers seeking favorable coverage, but it may also work out to their disadvantage and more or less block some of them from entering the news. And using media logic is always to some extent a risky affair, as the logic may also turn itself against organizations that are too eager. Seeking favorable coverage may concoct unfavorable outcomes.

8.2 Rules: barriers and opportunities

The media seek to fulfill their aims (making a living by publishing interesting and important news stories) on the basis of a number of more or less informal set rules. These rules sometimes serve as opportunities that can be exploited and will sometimes serve as barriers that prevent public service providers – and others – to enter the news on their own terms.

The most important informal rule for news stories is that they are generally simple and formulaic. The average news story offers, a critic would claim, a simplified and sensationalized take on an issue. Abstract and general policy issues are often reframed into personalized struggles between specific persons

126

(see Keane 2009: 98). The media run *endless stories*, as Herbert Gans observed, for instance about rugged individuals fighting faceless bureaucracies. This first rule is often a serious constraint for many public service providers as it may halt their important and interesting stories at the gates (the journalists) to the news or may propel them into quite predictable set stories of failing bureaucracies or third sector organizations spending most of their revenues on fundraising.

Many service providers experience that the media do not find their stories particularly newsworthy, as a survey on Australian third sector organizations for instance clarified (Maddison & Hamilton 2007). A good news story should be "timely, terse, easily described, dramatic, colorful and visualizable" (Cook 2005: 113); most of the stories that public and third sector service providers would like to tell do not fulfill these criteria. As a respondent notes: "Much of what we do is very technical and only accessible to a small audience", and another adds: "It seems they only want the really simple stories. The underlying issues are complex, and we strip away all that is complex." Public agencies need to reframe their issues when they want to communicate effectively through the media, as their "ordinary language is quite inappropriate for talking to the media". An experienced respondent describes how his organization deals with media inquiries:

"You need a simple explanation, in plain language, ludicrously short, based on fact, and able to be read out by someone who doesn't know a lot about the issue. It needs to be provided to any other minister. It is incredibly finely managed. It can seem like an entirely heart-breaking, Sisyphean task of rolling a rock back up a hill again, but if you don't attend to it, you end up in constant media chaos. If you don't manage these incidents, you can't go on with your truly important work."

In dealing with media queries, getting the words right is an incredibly important issue. It means the specific framing of the incident needs to go down well in a media story, something which for instance one CEO admits sometimes cost him a lot of time: "I spend a lot of time on getting the words right." One service provider described how they would use a communications agency to deal with the wordings and would deliberately hire the same bureau that was hired by the minister and his or her party in order to assure that they would be using the same language. And some other agencies described how they would often keep responses "very succinct", in order to leave journalists as little as possible on which to build or extend their stories.

Once service providers make it past the gatekeepers to the news, they often experience in bewilderment that they are portrayed in *recurring, one-sided*, or even utterly *hostile* frames. The frames may be recurring and one-sided, they are endless stories, which is sometimes very "dissatisfying" for service providers. A respondent notes how 90% of her media contact was on an issue that had been recurring since the 1970s. The organization had long since moved its focus to new issues, only to experience that journalists somehow cherished the existing issue and returned to them for the same commentary on a regular basis. They are thus always cast in "stereo-types" (Strömbäck 2008, 233), almost irrespective of what they want to communicate themselves. Earlier research on British executive agencies (quango's) also established how all media stories were more or less variations of the same story line of – in that case – ineffective and undemocratic governance structures (Deacon & Monk 2001a: 9). A respondent from a provider of community services described her sense of frustration with the cast and one-sided framing in the news:

"We'd love to have a good media report, but they always focus on the sensationalist bit. For instance, we had a good story on improving the community. But it turns out they keep showing old footage of kids sniffing petrol. It had been on file, was three years old, and that's just so frustrating! It's difficult to bring positive stories across because you still need to tag it back to some of the negative things going on."

Outright *hostile framing* is an issue specifically encountered by public service providers, who, in the focus groups, readily agreed they always needed to challenge the stereotype of the inefficient bureaucrat in the news (see also Cook 2005: 88). It is an uphill battle, as bureaucrats have less ability to speak and defend themselves in public. "Journalists", one of the respondents states, "seem to think that bureaucracy is ineffective, but that services are perfectible. So if a child dies, someone hasn't done his or her job very well; someone failed." In order to deal with this inbuilt hostile framing, one respondent notes how they would always "deal in specifics: it's a teacher, an engineer or a police man; not a bureaucrat".

Public service providers have little choice but to accept the type of framing journalists use in order to be able to produce important, interesting and 'selling' articles on a relatively regular basis. The only 'remedy' used by some service providers is to build warm, professional relations with journalists that allow them to challenge and alter their frames in the course of time. Journalists often need to write their stories very quickly – it is one of the reasons why the story-lines remain so similar in the course of time – and it is really helpful for organizations when they are the sources the journalist consults once (s)he needs to write a story. It is a practice that fosters respectful stories (the journalist will quite naturally be somewhat disinclined to nail down his or her source), it provides an opportunity to check, correct and put in 'facts', and it also means that there is a relationship that can be used in later stages to bring out positive stories and to correct the existing negative or one-sided stories. It also means that there is a relationship and some struggle between journalists and their subjects, described vividly by the respondent below:

"As a police officer you know that if you walk into the room, and there's a gun sitting on the table, whoever picks up the gun first has control over the room. So if you walk into the room

128

and you got the media running the gun, in other words they're taking charge of it and they're controlling the room and asking the questions. So when you're dealing with the media you must know what you got to say, and where you want the gun to be pointed, then you got the control over the room."

The news media write endless stories that are interesting and important, and in order to be able to do so, they usually use *established authorities*, such as politicians, as proxies for relevance. This is a rule that often works out to the detriment of public service providers who want to run stories in the news, as almost all media stories are triggered by statements of politicians; very few stories are triggered by government organizations or NGO's (Kepplinger 2002: 980). And once a politician has taken a stance, it is often undesirable and inappropriate (lest alone ineffective) for a public service provider or a contracted third sector organization to argue and respond, even though they may sometimes feel a strong inclination to do so. Some third sector organizations and the occasional public agency employed persons with an established news credibility, and they experienced how the media were always coming back to them with questions on relevant, task-related or just any issue. A CEO for instance notes how two of his staff "often participate in things, or on TV, not because they are from our organization, but they will show the brand then anyhow." Some third sector and public authorities also sensed that they would have a larger credibility in the news than politicians. "When it's a politician, media will naturally be more critical and hostile. They tend to think politicians are dishonest and self-serving. With us, they tend to assume we are serving the public interest."

A third rule, a rule that often works against public service providers, is the *conflict-rule*. Media tend to portray issues in terms of struggle and conflict. Tiffen (1999) for instance lists six types of common conflicts, that all have role-implications for both journalists and news-actors. As a result, many important issues receive little or no coverage, simply because "they were not controversial and did not lend themselves to a good story" (Weaver et al 2004: 271). The conflict rule is a real barrier for service providers whose work may be very technical and consist of individual stories that cannot be communicated in public. Also, most service providers are highly reluctant to become involved in politicized discussions, as they don't fancy the gamble of potentially upsetting their benefactors. "As long as you talk about facts", a respondent notes, "it's generally all right. But as soon as you get into 'what if's', and policy, you have to be very carefully managed ... It's a bit of a dancing game." In particular, public service providers eschew the situation where it's "politician versus bureaucrat" as this is an unfair battle that may also be punished in the aftermath of an issue, by cutting back resources for instance. Respondents note there is "frequent pressure" from journalists to enter into conflicts, "but we simply resist that". Speaking to the media thus requires that spokespersons, according to the same respondent, have the ability to "resist the urge to drift away from your well-informed position, understanding timely what journalists might want to do." Some respondents become really hesitant in dealing with the media, who "look for a simple, high profile story", as "the minute you say something, they build another fire into what you are saying". And another adds: "We are not in the position to offer running commentary on (…). Some politicians might want to do that, but we don't want to be a magnet for media interest."

The rules discussed so far are generally disadvantageous to service providers seeking favorable news coverage, although the rules are not cast in stone and can sometimes be exploited or amended. The next set of rules, however, can be quite helpful for service providers who want to communicate via the mass media (although there is no fail-safe and risk-free strategy).

The first potentially beneficial rule is the rule of *balanced reporting*. Journalists seek balanced reporting or, at least, want to be able to display both sides to a story. Public service providers are often called upon by journalists because they are needed as 'the other side' in an upcoming story. As a result, the organization will at least have the opportunity to have its say in public and may also be in a position to negotiate the overall direction of the story. A respondent from a third sector organization with a very specific purpose for instance notes how (s)he would attract a lot of media attention because there were not so many other people that could step in to bring balance to a story. The opportunity to speak brings the additional benefit that the organization may be able to change the course of events. A respondent for instance notes how they will sometimes refuse to go on in a show and how this sometimes helps to prevent a negative story from running, as the news media would need a second voice in order to have a balanced story. And another respondent adds how they will sometimes refrain from doing an interview, but will just issue a "clear statement, and if it's short enough, they need to use it, and repeat the one statement they have from you." The risk of this rule of course, is that an organization is tempted to offer a comment on an issue where they are "just needed to get a balanced story. They [the journalists] do that very often, and ask: 'couldn't you just say such and such?' But why would you?", a respondent warns, "you would only look like a goose?"

The second potentially beneficial rule is that, as the saying goes, *facts are sacred* in reporting. Journalists generally need facts to substantiate their stories, journalists also take research and facts quite seriously, and many public service providers are the producers and owners of a large share of the existing reliable data about public services. This 'competitive advantage' provides those public service providers with an opportunity to enter the news on their own terms or to make corrections in stories based on unreliable or disputed data. There are of course many stories that are not based on facts or that are based on rather foggy or forced excerpts from existing data sets. In practice, thus, journalists do not always live up to this high norm. But be that as it may, many public service providers are often asked to deliver facts to stories and they also deliberately produce research and data as means to generate favorable publicity. Earlier, Dalton and Wilson (2009) described how third sector organizations conduct or sponsor research, disseminate the findings via the media and may also assist journalists with statistics on request. The Australian respondents were very outspoken on the issue of how media coverage and research were strategically intertwined. The respondents for instance note that "it is always in our mind how to generate media attention from bits of (…) research that we do", that they "get mileage on some of the scientific stuff", and "we have started our own research, because in our field there's just opinions, and it's useful for the media and ministerial advisors". One of the respondents of a Dutch organization claimed that they had been doing strategic research now for four or five years, and generally managed to get media attention for their research, also because they invested in the quality of the research. And even though (s)he claimed to be quite selective in pursuing research projects, they would still be doing somewhere between 7 and 12 projects each year. All of these respondents underlined the importance of their media work. A respondent from a hospital for instance notes about the relevance of research for the media:

"Our strategy as a hospital is about building up a brand. It takes a lot of advocacy. We have cutting edge research and much works out very well [in the media]. If you can tie it to a case study, then they'll be interested. We bring up stories for instance on clinical excellence, high end surgery, and 'miracle' and 'worlds' first stories' on surgery. We want our experts to be out there commenting or talking about things. The media for instance love (…). So we have appointed a clinician on the issue, it's the first in the world. And really, it's just about the appointment of another clinician, but as it is the first in the world, the media just went crazy. But that's good for us. So they come all the time on all sorts of related issues. And we want them to come to us, whenever they write something about this particular issue."

The third beneficial rule for particularly third sector organizations is that celebrity news has become highly current. Using celebrities increasingly helps to sell newspapers and to attract audiences and listeners and, as if on the run, the celebrity might point the audience to the importance of the public service of a third sector organization. Some third sector organizations, particularly again in Australia, make active use of celebrities as a method of entering the news in favorable terms. Respondents note how they would "build a team of ambassador celebrities" and that there is "no better way to 'market' our things than through these persons and faces." A respondent from a large third sector organization for instance combines the two rules together and discusses how they would launch the outcomes of research projects in a media setting and use celebrities as well for promotion. Another respondent describes how they would use a "rugby player, or Nick Cave or Cate Blanchett, as a way to have the minister present as well."

The fourth and last potentially beneficial media rule is that good stories are often based on the *human face*. As service providers work with many of the people that are portrayed in media stories, and as they will have their contact details, they are often asked by journalists to 'produce' or fill in personal stories. Quite a few of the service providers admitted that they would routinely 'deliver' subjects for the press and for events. "The idea is", a communications officer explains, to "find personal stories that illustrate a general point". In order to do so, organizations may use some of their employees with "eye-catching occupations" (the Dutch respondent used the term "aaibaar"), or produce a "whole package, with the CEO and a patient in a home". One of the larger organizations for instance described how they had a pool of some 150 clients around the country who are all trained speakers and can be 'used' whenever an important issue comes up in the media. Providing personal stories is also an asset in battling and balancing some of the recurring negative stories. A respondent for instance describes:

> "We try to change the idea that homeless people are drunk old man, because they're generally not. So we will talk to clients about getting involved in the media. This is done under strict briefing rules and with a very short shelf life. … People must know: 'this could be your son or daughter'."

There was only one Australian third sector organization with regular client contacts that did not help journalists to produce a human face. "We generally stay out", the CEO of the organization noted, "because our clients have nothing to gain by it. Our clients are judged; stereotyped. The journalists haven't got the attention span to understand the complex situations our clients are in. Whenever they talk with us, they just want to have someone whom they can hold up in public." It is difficult to say whether their clients had more to fear from the media than some other clients or whether this cautious policy was due to personal or organizational preferences. The statement nevertheless points towards an important inherent risk in 'using' clients to provide the media with a human face: the client or the organization may be harmed by the publicity. There just is no certainty that what starts out as a positive news story will remain positive. Also, even the best trained client may stumble into all sorts of trouble in the course of an interview.

8.3 Production logics: chances and a major hazard

A final set of dimensions of media logic refers to the production logics – which often serve as enablers *and* constraints – of the news that may again be used by news-seeking service providers or may hamper them in their attempts.

The first of a set of four important production logics refers to the *scarcity of resources* of the media. This production logic is a formidable constraint for the media themselves and is critically important to the question of what the news is and how it is covered. The media need to crank out stories on a regular basis and have limited resources to accomplish the *daily miracle* of the news (Conley 2005). This timeless constraint has gained importance because of financial pressures and the high levels of competition between and across media. Whether it is factually correct or nor is difficult to substantiate, but almost all respondents agreed that the media operate with ever more limited resources and that this constraint offered public service providers opportunities that could sometimes be exploited quite easily. "They are all young and not well prepared", a respondent offhandedly summarizes. Others add that "they have no time", that "they are all overworked" and that "there are no more specialized journalists that know the area and know some context and history." At face value, the under-resourced reality of the current media is a risk for service providers as journalists are not able, in the eyes of the service providers, to produce balanced and comprehensive stories that take the proper context of a service into account. "The correspondent is twenty-three", a spokesperson claims, "and she always wants it tomorrow. There is no time to put it in context." The lack of journalistic resources, however, is easily converted into an advantage, as it provides service providers with the opportunity to use the media to run the stories they want themselves. They may "provide content", a respondent notes, or even "spoon-feed them the messages". "The story they run", a respondent notes, "is often the story you give them." Yet another respondent describes:

"The media seem so hungry for information that they take whatever you hand them. We pack it in with emotions and photographs, we do the visuals for the media that they can just run. They're quite restricted these days in the number of journalists they have operating on a given day. So if they can be handed information that is useable for them, and if it's a story and its good news, especially suburban, they generally keep printing whatever you give them. So we're thinking, 'as long as we keep pumping out good stories that fit the news and are informative to the community, they won't go looking for the negative stories'."

The high level of dependence of the media on content from service providers is neither a novelty nor specifically related to public service providers. McCombs (2004: 102-3; see also Weaver et al 2004: 270) for instance noted that nearly half of the stories in the quality press over the last twenty years were substantially based on information subsidies, such as press releases, from governments. And Gandy (1982) already noted that the American federal government employed more than three thousand people whose primary job it was to produce information subsidies for the media. A similar claim can be made here. Our research suggests that most large public service providers also aim to influence the news with a sophisticated mix of what essentially boils down to information subsidies. In addition, many of the third sector as well as some of the public sector respondents noted how they had formal or informal agreements with magazines to deliver content or to appear regularly in talkback radio or on TV. They would say that they would 'do' talkback radio once a month, "simply go on a Monday night as it is now, for about 20 or 30 minutes", or write articles and opinion pieces for newspapers or magazines.

The scarcity of resources is exacerbated by the second production logic, the intense *deadline pressure* that is customary to the trade of the news. Deadlines are normal, as the news is by definition always the last thing that happens and it needs to be reported ever faster in the 24-hour-newscycle. As a result, journalists will constantly need access to information, visuals, people, facts and other 'materials' on which to couch their stories and they need to be able to access these materials swiftly. This production logic is, again, a constraint which is potentially damaging to public service providers. It for instance persuades journalists to cast their stories in pre-fixed and sometimes negative frames, because that is the most efficient way of concocting a story. But the constraint can easily be converted into an organizational asset, as the responses from most respondents suggest. The bottom line is that under-resourced media ("they try to do more with less") often need bits of information on a very short notice and journalists will often rely on sources that have proven themselves to be beneficial and efficient. Some public service providers have established themselves as such entry points to information for journalists, something that gives them the opportunity to provide and control the data that the news media use. This, in turn, gives them the opportunity to air their own opinions and also gives them the possibility to challenge and perhaps change some of the self-evident, but perhaps partial or repetitive, frames in which news stories are often cast.

The best way to use the deadline pressure is by being a reliable aide to journalists who need to get their stories out quickly. Rule number one in this regard, and it was repeated almost unisono by all respondents, is to always be accessible. A CEO from a third sector organization for instance states:

> "If they know you are reliable, people [journalists] will come to you first. So that is important. If they would ring me at six o'clock in the morning or at ten o'clock at night, they knew that they would still get a response. Our media people are always on call."

Being accessible means you can help journalists with data and contacts, as "they often don't have contacts themselves", which of course implies that the organization has some control over what contacts are used in the 'construction' of news stories. Whether or not a service provider develops into an aide in the daily struggle with the deadline depends on the quality of the relationship that is developed. "Over time, once you establish a reputation, they will come to you", a respondent from a third sector organization describes. And another respondent adds: "And we always compliment the journalist, even when you're not very pleased with the fact that something came in the news, but we always say 'thank you for covering that issue fairly'. They really appreciate that." One of the ways to establish a good relationship with journalists is to employ them yourself. One respondent from a large service provider for instance noted: "We employ lots of journalists and they have good networks. They know how to spark interest in a story and we employ some fifty of these people, with a lot of networking, and us feeding them stories." The quality of the relationship also pays off in terms of coverage. A proficient working relationship with the media generates an increasing number of stories on one's organization, a respondent notes, and also makes the stories more positive. A CEO recalls: "The more open I am, the less hostile questions I get".

The third important production logic, that is really also a constraint, is the existence of predetermined *news holes* that basically need to be filled by journalists. The news hole refers to all the space that is left after the removal of the advertorial space and it can actually be measured (McCombs 2004: 27). Newspapers may for instance have two educations reporters that will run a more or less fixed number of stories on education each week. In addition, the different news outlets appear with metrical regularity. Almost irrespective of the events of the day, there are empty time slots to be filled for designated types of news, and there are specialized journalists looking for stories with a predictable (and high) regularity. There are, as one of the respondents states: "Just so many columns to fill". The strategic response to this fact is highly similar for all organizations operating in more or less newsworthy policy areas: "we", follows the same respondent from above "try to press news from anything". Many respondents spoke in similar and slightly cynical terms: "We are there to produce gist for the mill", or: "We have a method to ascertain that we appear in the news on a regular basis", and: "There is a space that needs to be filled, so you provide the content to fill it yourself." It echoes the famous words from the Blair-team: you have to feed the (media) beast.

The obvious advantage of filling the news hole yourself is that it ascertains that there are less negative stories. Some of the respondents understand this as a real competition between potential stories. "If we don't do it, someone else will, so there's a real competition". And another adds: "It's also explicit. They [the journalists] would say: we are going to run this on Sunday, unless you got something better ..." And a third respondent states:

"In our policy field, we deal in hope and fear. That's the choice. If you provide them [journalists] with something good, about real lives, with specifics, real people, and you tell it well, that is attractive to them and better than a story of fear."

This struggle over content between service providers and journalist can sometimes be quite explicit and outspoken. A number of Australian respondents described a very high level of planning of positive stories, particularly for salient public services operating close to the political center. One respondent for instance notes: "We have a target for the number of positive stories we want every week, with certain numbers of radio, TV, etcetera". And another respondent adds: "We have a strategy for the day; like on Tuesday we want this and on Wednesday that. We battle constantly to get into the media. There is always a plan, and we all agree it is a real battle."

These first three production logics are relatively easily exploited by public service providers. The fourth production logic, however, refers to the *editorial process* and is most readily understood as a barrier and as a major hazard for organizations trying to use the news media in order to distribute their messages. Service providers normally deal with individual journalists and, when they invest in the relationship with the person, they will oftentimes be able to at least have their say in the article and to correct some of the facts. On this level, given the large extent of operational freedom of reporters, the editorial process actually serves service providers (and others) quite well, as the process is highly transparent and as they deal with reporters with often very restricted up-to-date knowledge of a field. Most reporters will usually agree with pre-readings of their material and can be reached for discussion. Once the reporter has finished the story, however, a highly un-transparent post-production process evolves that may have severe and detrimental effects on the organizations in a story. A respondent describes:

"One of the things with the media is that you can have a great relationship with the journalist, but as soon as it leaves the journalist and goes to the sub editor, that person [the initial journalist, TS] has no more control over the story. You can have a great story with all the accurate information and then there is a headline that screams something completely contradictory to what your (...) messages are."

The same may happen on television, where lines from an interview can be cut and pasted, so that the intended message becomes embedded in a totally different story-line. For these reasons, there is no fail-safe way to engage with media as there is no way to ensure that the end result of the editorial process is not the opposite of one's intentions.

136

A telling example of what may happen comes from a Dutch government advisory council offering policy advice on a range of social policy issues. The media always sought to cast their reports in the frame of "expert body slams the minister". The council itself strove to keep its news items substantive and always shied away from open criticism of politicians. On one occasion, however, they published a report on the integration of ethnic minorities, describing how some policies were ineffective. In its press release, the council condensed the 170-page report to one telling example of ineffective policies, the "multicultural barbecue". The council claimed that those barbecues and similar short-lived projects – sympathetic as they arguably are – were ultimately ineffective in fostering stronger ties between people from different ethnic groups. The example worked quite well in the sense that most media found the report both important and interesting, and wrote about the story, even using the example. The council of course used the simple example as a device with which to bring a more complex issue to the attention of the general public. However, the story was first published in a newspaper, adjacent to a picture of the minister eating conspicuously non-white food with conspicuously non-white people. As a result, any person turning to this page of the newspaper got the same impression: a story in the "expert body slams the minister"-frame, even though nothing in the actual text of the story suggested this.

8.4 Media logic and public services in sum

The daily news is produced on the basis of a relatively stable set of rules, aims, production logics and constraints. These ingredients of media logic determine to a large degree which of the immeasurable number of daily events are successfully transformed into a news story. Mediatization implies that organizations adapt their own internal structures and processes in order to be able to cope with the essentially external logics and rules of the media. Furthermore, in their attempts to engender positive news stories, while simultaneously fending of the negative stories, public service providers can be seen to tussle with these rules, aims, productions logics and constraints of the media's logic. Some of the rules work to their advantage, and many service providers have learnt or are trying to find ways to exploit that advantage in terms of favorable news coverage. Some of the other rules stand as formidable barriers between the organization and their media aspirations. It leaves some organizations disillusioned with the press, has inspired some others to exploit the promises of the new (social) media, whereas a last group of organizations persists in attempts to work with the news media and to find ways of making it into the news on their own terms.

Table 8 below provides an overview of the most important aims, rules, production logics and constraints of the media.

Table 8: Media logic: aims, rules, production logics & constraints

Aims	Rules	Production Logics (Constraints)
• Newsworthy news: important and interesting stories • Economic goal: selling a product in order to be able to make news or to make a profit	• Endless stories (set frames) • Established (news) authorities • Conflict rule • Balanced reporting • Sacred facts • Celebrity (and soft) news • Human face to stories	• Scarce resources • Intense deadline pressures • Pre-determined news-holes • Editorial process and post-production

This chapter has investigated how the logic of the news media affects public service providers trying to create or avoid publicity. It has been largely analytical and it aimed to understand the *practices* of public organizations engaging with media. Whether these practices are at all desirable from a normative perspective, and whether these practices come with risks for the organization at large, has been left out of the equation. These issues will be addressed in the next and final chapter of this book.

9. Organizational mediatization: playing with matches

"The thing is, if you want to use the media, you need to know that if you play with fire you might get burnt. So we always counsel to be careful. To the extent that you think of the media as a tool for your own exploitation, I think you invite the potential for it to turn, where they ask 'what are you doing? You're just manipulating us and spinning us for your own purposes.' And that's what a lot of people do."

Public organizations spend considerable resources on following, anticipating, adapting to and communicating with the news media. For larger service providers, particularly for those working in politically salient fields, the news media are a constant companion. The news media embody an enticing promise for organizations: positive news stories are expected to have a large and broad impact on their reputations, their external relations and, not in the last place, on executive and staff morale. Pressured, transforming and ambitious public service providers will often increase their investments (time, attention, staff, and technologies) in media-related work in hopes of improved news coverage with a positive spin off in their policy fields. Many service providers have also learnt to integrate media communication in their core functions of service provision. But investing in media-related work is not a failsafe strategy. Organizations can't control the outcomes of their exchanges with journalists. "In order to use it", a CEO notes, "you must dare to take the risk".

"Using" the "risky" media is like playing with matches, a metaphor brought forward by several respondents and on different occasions. The news media can be essential in attaining certain goals and it is oftentimes exhilarating, but there is always a risk that operating with the media sparks off a large and uncontrollable fire. 'Fire' stands as a metaphor for a variety of potential negative consequences of media strategies-gone-wrong. Failures and incidents may be damaging for the people involved, may have a severe impact on an organization's strategic position and they could also affect the services the organization provides to citizens.

This chapter will discuss some of the most critical consequences of the mediatization of public service providers. Before turning to those consequences, however, some reflection is required on the process of mediatization, the driving forces behind the process and on some of the important variations between organizations.

9.1 Mediatization: the process in short

'Mediatization' has become a trending topic in political communications research. The number of recent mediatization-publications is staggering; and there is certainly more to come. The vogue in mediatization studies signals the versatility of the concept. Its core idea: institutional adaptation to another institution's logic, has been found to be useful in a large number of hugely different studies. Conceptual versatility, however, often comes at a costly price. Conceptual overstretch then serves to obscure, rather than illuminate, important insights and research findings, and the apparent conceptual congruence masks over substantive incongruence underneath.

Against the backdrop of the recent boost in mediatization studies, and informed by warnings about the 'relevance' of the process as such (see Livingstone 2009; Schulz 2004), this book has sought to analyze organizational mediatization from a programmatically *empirical* perspective; using and refining some conceptual distinctions that were successfully introduced in the literature. This book is the reflection of what in essence was a *fact finding mission*. The underlying research project cast a wide net and combined a number of different research methods, in order to sketch a comprehensive portrait of the mediatization of organizations providing public services. The relevance of this endeavor follows from its consequences for service providers and from the relative novelty of the subject. While there is a bulging pile of studies on the mediatization of the central actors in democracies – political parties, governments and parliaments – there has been only scant academic attention for these more peripheral but, in their consequences for citizens, hugely important service providers. If anything, this book hopefully helps to underline the relevance of the issue, as it has shown how public service providers now occupy a substantial niche in the daily news, how they spend considerable resources – directly and indirectly – on media-related work and how they all in some ways integrate the demands from their media environments in their strategies and activities.

Mediatization has been understood and described in this book as a response to – real or imagined – media pressure. Critical journalists, negative editorials, pack journalism, and investigative journalism, are all real forms of media pressure. However, organizations can be found to mediatize even in those cases where journalists are not actually "digging" for stories and the press does not provide a great deal of coverage. The anticipation of, positive or negative, media coverage is what drives mediatization; rather than the level and negativity of reporting in any real sense. Telling of this is how almost all respondents in our research thought that their organizations and policy fields received large shares of the media's attention, even though there were enormous differences in actual reporting on their organizations. The media, thus, do exert their pressure collectively, as an institution, rather than individually, through specific queries or publications.

Mediatization in general relates to institutional adaptation – here: of service providers – to the institutional logic of the media – here: the news media. Mediatization means that organizations adapt their internal structures and processes to the 'logics' of the media. The media work with a number of set rules for relevance, importance, timing, and framing of issues. The media also produce the news on the basis of a set of production logics and constraints. Organizations are adapting to the media's logic whenever they adapt their own communications to the demands of journalists and editors. Their adaptation is even more complete, when they also incorporate the media rules for relevance and importance in their own operations, for instance by substituting their own policy rules for what is important according to the media.

Organizational mediatization has been analyzed in this book with an analytical device that is essentially a 'three-by-three'. Three dimensions of mediatization (accommodation, amalgamation and substitution) have been studied in three consecutive phases in the 'production process' of public policies (inputs, throughputs, and outputs). Organizational *accommodation* refers to the rules, structures and processes that enable organizations to operate effectively in their media environments. Media monitoring services, media training, codes of conduct, communications departments, media aides and strategic marketing, are all forms of organizational accommodation. Organizational *amalgamation* refers to the mingling of media-related activities with essentially non-media activities. Where the processes of actual service provision become intertwined with media communication, or where senior strategic staff is constantly aware of and alerted about media reporting, the customary internal processes and concerns for the external media environment amalgamate. Organizational *substitution*, finally, refers to all those cases where organizations choose to pursue goals via the media that were previously pursued with other means. Some CEOs exemplified, for instance, how they would use media interviews as means with which to inform their employees about impending organizational restructurings. And quite a few service providers used media communication as a cog in the wheel of effective service delivery, for instance for raising the public's awareness for issues, fostering active citizen participation or as a powerful investigative tool.

9.2 Researching organizational mediatization: some critical reflections

The central empirical chapters of this book (5-7) have sought to provide a comprehensive overview of the mediatization of public service providers. These chapters all concluded with tables providing overviews of the most important aspects and indicators of mediatization. These indicators, however, need to be handled with care in future research and can in and of itself not automatically be interpreted as signs of mediatization. The point – and from a researcher's perspective: the trouble – is that the process of organizational mediatization does not follow a fixed trajectory along historically stable indicators. Organizations mediate in different ways, so to speak. In order to handle their media environments, some organizations for instance choose to centralize all public communication and to restrict media communication to just the CEO and his or her spokespersons. Some other organizations, conversely, will chose to spread 'public speaking' along a number of specialists and may even try to keep their chief executive in a low media profile. The underlying goal, our respondents suggested, is that all organizations strive to maximize the effectiveness of their public performances, they just choose different institutional embodiments. This suggests that the indicators of organizational mediatization are *situational,* dependent on the people involved, their past experiences and the intricacies of a given service and policy field.

Furthermore, the indicators for mediatization are also *historical.* Specific organizational forms will 'work' in a given period of time but may lose (or gain) relevance over the years. An example of this process is the – now – traditional press release. Our comparative analysis suggested that the organizations who were most actively using their websites as aides to journalists in the production of news, simultaneously issued less press releases than other organizations. This evidence suggests that web 2.0 technology and social media are now giving public organizations new, and more effective, tools with which to gain access to the news. The organizations relying on the standard press release are often laggards in the process of mediatization.

A further challenge to the researchers of organizational mediatization is that it is neither a stable, nor an inevitable or irreversible process. Mediatization is not stable, in the sense that it is not unidirectionally evolving in clearly marked and escalating steps. Mediatization may evolve with stops and starts. And mediatization is not irreversible in the sense that organizations will necessarily become ever more mediatized over time. Whereas increasing levels of mediatization are likely on the level of 'populations', surely individual organizations may "demediatize" as well and revert to their independence from the media as an institution. And demediatization is not necessarily ineffective. Mediatization is thus, overall, not an inevitable process and, even where it exists, a multifaceted process.

A further obstacle in our understanding of mediatization regards the *direction of causation*. Mediatization studies always explore how one institution – in this book: public service providers – adapt and transform themselves in response to the pressure from the media as an institution. These studies rely, explicitly or implicitly, on unidirectional theories of causation. It is, according to the default theory, the media that changes how the other organizations operate; public service providers are then, almost by definition, portrayed as merely passive victims of external colonization. However, given the permanent mutual interactions, struggles and exchanges of personnel between media and the public sector, and given the advanced state of institutional fatigue of the traditional news media, this unidirectional theory of causation is not overwhelmingly convincing. For politics-media relationships, above all, a model of mutual adaptation and influencing is more persuasive. Respondents in our research pointed in the same direction, for instance when relating how they would often coproduce stories with the media, background journalists on issues or help journalists to track down experts or 'victims'. These are all signs of mutual adaptation, or, if we want to mirror Mazzoleni & Schulz's (1999: 249) famous dictum of the mutagenic effect of mediatization, signs of *mutual mutagenesis*. Mediatization should accordingly be understood as a mutual adaptation process between two institutions actively trying to gain influence on the other in which both, at least theoretically, could gain the upper hand. A respondent from one of the service providers directly alluded to this combative character of mediatization: "We try to change the rules but we are beaten at it all the time."

A final note regards the *historical* heart of the concept of mediatization. As the term clearly signifies, 'mediatization' aims to describe a process of historical transformation. This book, and many other mediatization studies for that matter, is however only marginally or partially historical in focus. Rather, many studies are in fact more concerned with the (utterly unutterable) actual mediatiz*edness* of – here – public organizations, rather than with their gradual mediatiz*ation*. It would be interesting for future research to focus more specifically on the moment of actual organizational adaptation in response to the media. This would do justice to the essentially historical character of the concept. Furthermore, tracing the moment or period of change, would also further our understanding of its driving forces. The standard theoretical assumption would be that mediatization is a more or less rational *response* to media pressures which gains wind through technological advances. It is essentially an *ecological* theory of change, expecting, as was common in the history of organization theory, structural change to be functional in the sense of making organizations survive – or even flourish – in their competitive environments. Whether this is actually the case for the mediatization of public organizations is however an unresolved question.

At least one different explanation of patterns in historical change is available and seems, at face value, tempting. Mediatization could also 'just' be a case of *institutional isomorphism*. Institutional isomorphism is a general theory that explains change and homogeneity of organizational structures from the shaping forces of governments and professions (DiMaggio & Powell 1983). The theory contends that efficiency is in general at the back of the heads of managers making decisions about how to structure their organizations. However, as they write, they are "more concerned with the menu of possible options that managers consider". And on this menu of options are the choices that have been made by colleagues, role models and competitors. The menu necessarily consists of a limited set of institutional design principles that seem to be inevitable in a given period of time because they are simply customary. The mechanism of change is then in part the process of repeating earlier decisions. Organizational change, and organizational mediatization, could well be a process of copying and mimicking others' prior decisions.

It matters a great deal whether organizational mediatization is a process of rational adaptation or of institutional isomorphism. If it a case of adaptation, it is accordingly more or less inevitable for organizations to mediatize in order to survive and to be successful. The policy-implications of this view should be clear: there is little reason to question the mediatization of public services as such and 'more' can be easily equaled with 'better'. If mediatization, however, is driven by contingent decisions by managers and CEOs in public organizations who are basically copying and re-taking previous decisions, if mediatization is a case of institutional isomorphism, the policy implications are the exact opposite. This would make a strong case for a critical and self-reflective examination of the merits of mediatization for public services. Are strongly mediatized organizations more, or less, likely to serve their causes and missions properly, for instance? And, are strongly mediatized organizations more, or less, likely to operate and exist effectively over time? The answer to questions about the gross merits of mediatization, and the factors explaining its course of events, must be left for future research. We will now refocus our attention on the findings from current research, and critically discuss variations in mediatization and the effects of the process.

9.3 Organizational mediatization: variations

Organizational mediatization has been described in general terms in this book. The analysis has not been directed at our understanding of existent variations but rather at our understanding of overarching patters. The quasi-uniformity of the language and descriptions in this book should not hide, however, that there are numerous variations in levels of mediatization, relating to organizational forms and capacities. Four sources of variation stand out in relevance: resources, organizational type, competition, and strategy.

Resources

A first factor explaining levels of mediatization is the availability of resources. Engaging with the media is to some degree an issue of resources in the sense that people must be allowed the time to engage with the media and that media specialists simply need to be hired. A respondent from a smaller service provider "running on the smell of an oily rag", for instance indicated that media monitoring was not an option for them. Gaining a media profile and working effectively with the media requires a level of media skill and professionalization that may be beyond the grasp of small service providers, although the ability to do well in the media is for born performers a "gift of life". "Only the big third sector organizations will be able to participate effectively in the media", another respondent notes, "because of the availability of resources".

Many respondents in this research pointed out that media skills and media awareness are not naturally available in organizations providing public services. They would indicate that many people are not naturally good at dealing with the media, that many public organizations will not have the funding to do so, or that organizations should resist the inclination to redirect their revenues from the services to media-related work. Working with the media can be beneficial, but often requires resources that could be used to serve other ends. A respondent from a slightly uncharacteristic public service provider for instance pointed out that they had a "massive 12 million Australian dollar marketing budget." And a CEO from a successful third sector organization pointed out:

> "I came in 2000, and we built from there on the basic premise that if people don't know who you are or what you do, they can't give to you. So for us profiling the organization, gaining media exposure, has been absolutely critical in our growth. We have been doubling our income consistently for ten years. The board ... took the risk of investing in a full time person and it turned out as a good example of that if you put a good resource in, you see the benefits this accrues, and we have seen a hike in our income."

The quote above signifies that resources are not absolutes, not fixed entities, and that investments in media people and media strategies may sometimes (sometimes!) pay off in terms of the acquisition of more support and funding. Some other respondents provided vivid examples of how their media strategies paid off in terms of success and increased funding. Nevertheless, the availability of resources and, hence, organizational size, is an important factor shaping the extent to which organizations are able to adjust to their media environments.

Organizational types

A second, major factor explaining variance in levels of mediatization is the public-private dichotomy used in this book. Public service providers, particularly those working close to the government, have become considerably more mediatized than third sector organizations providing public services on either a permanent basis or on temporary contracts. This should not come as a surprise, of course, as they work so close to the political-administrative center on which the media traditionally focus the gist of their attention. More interestingly, however, an analysis of different types of organizations reveals two apparent paradoxes.

The first paradox relates to the real and perceived levels of media pressure on various types of service providers. Our analysis of the media pressure on service providers in terms of numbers of news stories revealed that the real pressure on third sector organizations was, in comparison, considerably lower. This was, again, no real surprise. Surprising and more paradoxical was the finding that our respondents, irrespective of this fact, experienced a largely similar level of media pressure. This paradox confirms that media pressure is experienced more in terms of anticipation than in terms of real reporting. The paradox can furthermore be understood when the variations in *types of stories* are taken into account. The type of news stories was found to differ between public and third sector organizations. Whereas public service providers are the subjects of a large number of thoroughly neutral media stories, the media coverage of third sector organizations is generally more outspoken: they are the subjects of considerably more positive as well as more negative news stories.

The second paradox is that public service providers were more strongly mediatized in the first phases (inputs and throughputs) whereas third sector organizations were more mediatized in terms of integrating media in their outputs. On the level of the mediatization of organizational inputs and throughputs it was apparent that public organizations were able to set of more resources for media monitoring and the accommodation of organizational processes. Some respondents from third sector organizations described how they would listen and read the media in a different way after they had acquired government contracts. The news

146

had just become more relevant. Nevertheless, the level of media monitoring of third sector organizations was for most of them still curbed and found to be at a lower level. On the level of outputs, third sector organizations were found to use the media more strategically and openly than public service providers would (and perhaps could). They would speak candidly about marketing and branding and about polishing their reputation. They would also make more active use of their websites in order to maximize the exposure of their messages. These findings all suggest that mediatization for third sector organizations is to a large degree a strategic choice. This strategy aims to establish credibility and commitment from stakeholders and, ultimately, intends to ascertain the survival of the organization and, more importantly, its mission.

Competitive pressures

A third factor affecting the mediatization of service providers, implicit already in the case above, is competitive pressure. Particularly in the third sector, some respondents relate the issue of using the media to the heavy competition between the many organizations operating in the same 'market'. Promoting your organization is then essential in order to elevate one's organization above its competitors for government assignments, grants or private donations. A CEO for instance sighs and notes that "the trouble is, if there's 1900 of these organizations around, how to be visible and in some meaningful way influential?" The recent trend of governance, in which executive tasks have been shifted around and moved to other sectors than the strict public sector, has brought this element of competitive pressure into the public sector. Government agencies must openly, or sometimes more covertly, compete for tasks and budgets with other public organizations, but also with challengers from the private sector. This is a driving force for mediatization, as one's media image and reputation can be helpful, as many respondents suggest, in the acquisition of tasks (and funding).

Strategy

The final factor explaining variance in mediatization is organizational strategy. Some organizations are actively and explicitly 'using' the media as strategic tools to enhance their goals while some others primarily strive to prevent negative stories. A wide variety of approaches to the media were found to exist. Some organizations were risk-taking and embracing new opportunities while others were more risk averse. An interesting example comes from governmental responses to the advance of social media. The Dutch ministry of the interior started *encouraging* government employees to use social media professionally in 2010. In Australia, on the contrary, many public and third sector organizations actually *forbade* their people to do so. A respondent explains: "People see Facebook as a personal photo album and don't realize it is a publication. Our people need permissions and I generally check."

This distinction between organizations trying to 'use' or trying just to 'handle and live with' the media mirrors a distinction earlier made by Richard Sennett. In writing about the 'flexible economy', he pointed out that there is a major distinction between employees who *choose* to become more flexible (like ICT professionals, in his example, often refraining from collective agreements and permanent contracts) and manual workers (drifting in and out of short-term jobs) who are *forced* to do so because permanent contracts are simply out of their reach. The first group of people are actively becoming more flexible while the second group is passively adapting. In a similar vein it could be argued that some organizations are *becoming mediatized*; they suffer from the pressure of the news media and search for solutions that help to alleviate that pressure. Other organizations are actively mediatizing; finding and implementing ways to integrate the opportunities of the media into their everyday operations and strategies.

Active strategies of mediatization have a profound impact on organizations. For many CEOs and managers, the media can be a critical asset in larger transformations and for realizing the organization's mission. It remains to be seen whether active media strategies are in fact supportive of goal accomplishment and successful change. Nevertheless, many CEOs and strategic officials were strongly convinced that it was, and they would provide arguments and examples in case. The mediatization of organizations can of course also have adverse effects on public service organizations. The next section of this book will discuss the most important, real and imaginary risks, of mediatization for public service providers.

9.4 Mediatization: real and imaginary risks

Mediatization is a process of institutional adaptation which means that institutions change into something they previously were *not*. The pressing question is then whether the organization has evolved into a *new and improved* version of its self or whether the organization has simply lost sight of its 'true self'. Numerous respondents thought that their own organization was using the media appropriately: the media helped them serve their goals and they had not been making compromises to their true mission. Interestingly, however, many respondents opined that quite a few of their colleagues and competitors had not managed to find this neat balance. Their competitors suffered in various ways from the adverse effects of mediatization. Some of those effects regard their organizations, some of those effects regard their strategic relations with the government, and some were more personal.

Mission creep

A first potential adverse organizational effect of over-adaptation to media is *mission creep* (Shergold 2009). Organizations, aiming to please their principals and aiming to shine in the media, may lose track of their real purpose and mission. This risk most strongly relates to third sector organizations, whose missions are unrelated to the government, once they start working for the government. Choosing to provide public services on the basis of directives or funding from the government may compromise their causes. Hamilton & Maddison (2007) have for instance described how working on government contracts reins in their opportunities for advocacy. Working for the government simply makes it more difficult to criticize the government and many respondents recognized this issue or suggested that this was the reason why they were hesitant to accept public funding. Other respondents would in contrast, even though they admitted they had to bite their lips at times, raise the pragmatic counterargument that access to policy networks might be more important than advocacy, as it enabled them to influence policies in a more subtle but more effective way. Different approaches may thus be successful. Irrespective of the practical merits of various approaches, however, the real issue remains whether media-related work actually helps organizations attain goals they originally wanted to obtain or leads to goal displacement and mission creep.

Corporate narcissus

Organizations operating with a high media profile, organizations cultivating their reputations in the mass media, may easily become obsessed and self-absorbed. Like corporate Narcissuses falling in love with their own reflections. None of the respondents in our research thought they had fallen for this risk themselves (of course), most of the respondents would readily concede that many others in their branch had. It would be difficult to pass the verdict of 'self-absorbed' on academic grounds. However, the research for this book clearly demonstrates how larger public organizations are strongly aware of their media environment and that reputational issues are extremely important to their executives. It is, as Cook (2005: 149) already described, that service providers "are all concerned with making news, not merely because they are willing to react to reporters but because it serves their political and policy interests at the same time inside and outside of their agencies." It is a thin line from here to cross to the situation where image is everything (and service becomes secondary). It is an allegation that, again, did not hold true for our respondents but that was easily observed in many others, ministers in particular:

> "Ministers surround themselves with bright young things. They're not long out of school, they're so young. One has a twenty-two year old advisor, with no specific knowledge. Their job description is: 'make the minister look better'. They advise on speeches from the perspective of how the tabloid would pass it; and will it pass the 'Allen Jones test' (a famous Australian radio-host, TS)?"

Risk aversity

Organizations who, like Narcissus, fall in love with their own projected image are among the more offensive specimen. Many other organizations, however, rather become *risk averse* under the pressure of the media. External pressures may, as Behn (2001: 30) stated so eloquently, "turn the timid into cowards and the bald into outlaws". Risk aversity is good in one sense, as it shies many service providers away from all sorts of potentially harmful and unsuccessful endeavors. On the other hand, however, risk averse organizations also risk being unsuccessful, as they may be afraid of taking necessary but difficult decisions. Again, people didn't see these issues in their own organizations, but clearly noted them in others:

> "We were not scared of the media either. I don't think we could have been as successful as we were if we had been scared of it. I observed others being scared. They wouldn't want to put their heads up, wouldn't want to be different. We thought we needed to, and I knew there were going to be reports and somebody would make a negative statement. It never prevented us from doing a thing, as I saw happening with others."

Blame shifting

The propensity to respond risk aversely to media pressure is understandable and rational, as service providers need to cope with their specific vulnerabilities in encounters with the media. For one reason, service providers operate in environments where politicians launch regular criticisms of bureaucracies and agencies. And those bureaucracies and agencies are often simply unable to defend themselves publicly in equal terms. They may be formally prohibited from responding to politicians' claims. Contracted service providers may work under "gagging clauses", as a respondent described them, which halt them from speaking publicly about the issue. And service providers face a rather dim chance of success when clashing with a politician. The trouble, from the service provider's perspective, is furthermore that they are often, as a Dutch respondent highlighted, "the last in the chain, where faults become visible, so you are easily blamed." And an Australian counterpart followed up in a similar way: "Our staff faces the consequences of policies. Things that go wrong end at our organization ... It is a major communicative task, to counter these types of allegations."

In the public administration literature it is common to list 'blame shifting' under the informal goals behind the delegation of a task to others (Hood 2002), such as, in our case, more or less autonomous service providers and third sector service providers. Many respondents underlined the veracity of that analysis and one of them even stated: "We're there to some degree to spare politicians to do things they rather not do". And another respondent provided a telling example of blame shifting, where the service provider became a lightning rod for criticism:

"We had a totally different story on (...) that became national. (...) It was transformed from this tiny little issue into a national and even international debate on sexualization of children. It lingered on in today's show. The one who popped up [on TV] was the principal. Everyone, the minister, the Director General, the regional director, no one wanted to come anywhere near it. So they left it to the principal of the small school to answer, basically left it to the person most unable to delegate it to anybody else. It was deliberately kept at a local level, kept at a distance from government. We (the government's media people, TS) prepped the principal. The poor (...) did a wonderful job. Had it been great news from the school, the minister would have taken it. That's how it works, and to be fair, that's accepted."

Centralization

A second major intra-organizational effect is that mediatization further strengthens the centralization within government as well as between government and service providers. What starts out as the coordination and integration (at a central level) of public speaking, evolves into outright organizational integration in the sense that the executive organization is tied to the government as its final owner, benefactor or donor. The centralization starts out on the premise that service providers "take extreme care not to piss of the minister". They will, even when they speak critically in public, "be very careful to avoid putting the minister in an awkward position." Press releases will be pre-run through the government's office, or the service provider "would ring you up and talk to you to check in advance". It makes it "more difficult to lobby in this situation, as you can't always easily go out on the street to protest and it happened I decided not to comment on issues that touched on our work".

Most public service providers pointed out that their autonomy to operate in the media was limited to the effect that they should not harm the government. Most third sector organizations raised a similar point, stating "I wouldn't be critical on the government under our logo because they're our funder." However, it can be difficult to differentiate speaking out on the basis of one's mission and expertise from 'pissing of the government'. A researcher from a public agency for instance described just how thin that line is:

> "As a climate scientist, I might inform (the media, TS) that the lifetime of carbon dioxide in the atmosphere means that the only way of stabilizing global climate is by reducing emissions by 50% in 2050 and by 80% by 2080. In the current environment, that is seen as commenting on the government policy of not setting reduction targets." (quoted from Lowe 2007: 63)

Punishment

Organizations who miss-time their media launches – or time it correctly and just choose to collide head on with the current government – will face the risk of retribution. Contracts may not be renewed, budgets may be cut and executives may not be reappointed (see also Aulich et al 2010). Respondents for instance claimed: "Some people might not be reappointed because they annoy government so much through the media", and "we're absolutely certain that some (appointments) haven't been renewed. One hundred percent certain. But it's not officially outspoken. But we all agree that after annoying [the government] for some time – they'd be serial offenders – they would be cut off." The same goes for budgets: "It can be difficult; the new government cut our funding by forty percent. The budget can be a form of retribution, it's the price you pay for independence and you must be robust enough to not be fearful". In the end, a respondent claims: "You know, elephants have long memories and governments do not forgive."

9.5 Playing with matches

Some of the risks of mediatization discussed above are real, in the sense that research and our respondents were able to provide telling examples of their materialization. Some of the other risks discussed are rather of an imaginary nature, such as mission creep. It is a profound risk for organizations, some people are vividly aware of it and it has been discussed by practitioners and academics alike, but it's existence is plainly difficult to establish. Nevertheless, future research may reveal that those imaginary risks are all too real and that public organizations may suffer from their effects. These may be some of the unintended consequences of the mediatization of public organizations. As noted before, media-related work is very much like playing with matches. The metaphor is important in more than just the most obvious sense of its meaning.

Obviously, the metaphor denotes that failures in handling the media may impose real losses on public service providers. The organizations may, just as the child with the matches in the metaphor, suffer from burns. The previous section highlighted some of the potentially severe burn wounds public organizations might suffer: the loss of their autonomy, punishment, mission creep or sheer ineffectiveness. The second implication of the matches-metaphor, however, points to a different implication. Matches sometimes come in handy or can even be indispensable for some causes. When handled with care and judgment, matches can be rather helpful in getting a job done that would otherwise, in our daily lives, be nearly impossible. The same goes for the mediatization of organizations. A certain level of it is simply of crucial importance for public organizations. Public services who operate without understanding of the daily news, without sufficient sensitivity for what in the media's eye constitutes a problem or without the ability to explain their measures and decisions in plain language, can be easily rendered obsolete. The media, however, also provide a *lure* to public organizations. It is exciting to interact with the media and to try to have one's story or view on an issue published in the news. This is not dissimilar from the kid in the metaphor who perhaps fully knows it is unwise to light the matches in certain places but simply can't resist the temptation. And this temptation makes that the negative effects of the matches (and, by implication, of mediatization), can easily take precedence.

Our research touched on a large number of cases where people in public services suffered in real terms from their encounters with the media. In effect, as a respondent notes, "some senior civil servants would much rather have their arm eaten of than appear on radio. Some of our media people have basically been begging, preparing talking points, really holding their hands, but some of them just won't do it." When solicited publicity goes wrong – or when service providers suddenly find themselves in the epicenter of a media storm – the impact on the organization and on individuals is quite intense. "It can leave a community traumatized for years", a respondent recalls, and "it's a body blow if you have been at the center of attention." The effect may be that people who were involved "won't speak to the media, even if it's on the local sports edition. They're terrified, they run miles to avoid the press". The impact is often most strongly in smaller organizations or communities, where critical media scrutiny is not their daily experience. "There is often a high sense of pride in smaller entities", a respondent analyzes, and the media story is then felt as "a personal attack. They feel they have let the community down and they will be gun-shy with the media afterwards".

The child in the matches-metaphor needs to learn to restrain him- or herself and needs to learn how to handle this exciting but dangerous device. The same goes for organizations providing public services in media-saturated societies. "It can be tricky", a CEO notes, "there are lots of downsides to it, little gains. It's safer to stay out, and if you don't do well, you're in deep strife, real trouble." The net balance of these pro's and con's, the question whether service providers have now learnt to handle this dangerous device appropriately or whether they keep falling for the temptation and are made to suffer, must be left for future research.

References

Alford, J. (2009). *Engaging Public Sector Clients. From Service-Delivery to Co-Production*. New York, NY: Palgrave MacMillan.

Altheide, D., & R. Snow (1979). *Media logic*. Beverley Hills, CA: Sage Publications.

Arnold, R.D. (2004). *Congress, the Press and Political Accountability*. New Jersey, NJ: Princeton University Press.

Asp, K. (1990). Medialization, media logic and mediarchy. *Nordicom-Review*, *11*, 47-50.

Aulich, C., H. Batainah, & R. Wettenhall (2010). Autonomy and Control in Australian Agencies. Data and Preliminary Findings from a Cross-National Empirical Study. *Australian Journal of Public Administration*, *69*, 214-228.

Auslander, P. (1999). *Liveness. Performance in a Mediatized Culture*. New York, NY: Routledge.

Barker, G. (2007). The public service. In: C. Hamilton & S. Maddison, *Silencing Dissent. How the Australian government is controlling public opinion and stifling debate* (pp. 124-147). Crows Nest, Australia: Allen & Unwin.

Barns, G. (2005). *Selling the Australian Government. Politics and propaganda from Whitlam to Howard*. Sydney, Australia: UNSW Press.

Behn, R.D. (2001). *Rethinking Democratic Accountability*. Washington, DC: Brookings Institution Press.

Bekke, H., & N. van Gestel (2004). *Publiek verzekerd. Voorgeschiedenis en start van het Uitvoeringsinstituut Werknemersverzekeringen (UWV) 1993-2003*. Apeldoorn, Netherlands: Garant.

Besley, T., & R. Burgess (2001). Political agency, government responsiveness and the role of the media. *European Economic Review*, *45*, 629-640.

Bevir, M., R.A.W. Rhodes & P. Weller (2003). Traditions of governance. Interpreting the changing role of the public sector. *Public Administration*, *81*, 1-17.

Blumler, J.G., & D. Kavanagh (1999). The Third Age of Political Communication. Influences and features. *Political Communication*, *16*, 209-230.

Boom, J. (2010). *Als een nacht met duizend sterren. Oorlogsjournalistiek in Uruzgan*. Amsterdam, Netherlands: Podium / BKB.

Brandsen, T., M. Oude Vrielink, T. Schillemans, & E. van Hout (2010). Nonprofit Organizations, Democratization and New Forms of Accountability. A

Preliminary Evaluation. In: S.P. Osborne & A. Ball, *Social Accounting and Public Management. Accountability for the Common Good* (pp. 90-102). London, UK: Routledge.

Brants, K., & P. van Praag (2005). *Politiek en media in verwarring. De verkiezingscampagnes in het lange jaar 2002*. Amsterdam, Netherlands: Het Spinhuis.

Brenchley, F. (2003). *Alan Fels. A Portrait of Power*. Milton, MA: Wiley & Sons.

Carpenter, D. (2002). Groups, the Media, Agency Waiting Costs, and FDA Drug Approval. *American Journal of Political Science, 46*, 490-505.

Christensen, T., & P. Lægreid (2011a). *The Ashgate research Companion to New Public Management. Autonomy And Regulation. Coping with Agencies in the Modern State*. Cheltenham, UK: Edward Elgar.

Christensen, T., & P. Lægreid (2011b). Democracy and administrative policy. Contrasting elements of New Public Management (NPM) and post-NPM. *European Political Science Review, 3*, 125-146.

Clayman, S., & J. Heritage (2002). *The news interview. Journalists and public figures on the air*. Cambridge, UK: Cambridge University Press.

Commissariaat voor de Media (2009). *Mediamonitor. Mediabedrijven en mediamarkten 2009*. Hilversum, Netherlands: CvdM.

Conley, D. (2005). *The Daily Miracle. An Introduction to Journalism*. Melbourne, Australia: Oxford University Press.

Considine, M. (1996). Market Bureaucracy? Exploring the Contending Rationalities of Contemporary Administrative Regimes. *Labor and Industry, 7*, 1-28.

Considine, M., & J.M. Lewis (2003a). Networks and interactivity. Making sense of front-line governance in the United Kingdom, the Netherlands and Australia. *Journal of European Public Policy, 10*, 46-58.

Considine, M., & J.M. Lewis (2003b). Bureaucracy, Network, or Enterprise? Comparing Models of Governance in Australia, Britain, the Netherlands, and New Zealand. *Public Administration Review, 63*, 131-140.

Cook, T. (2005). *Governing with the News. The News Media as a political Institution*. Chicago / London, IL/UK: University of Chicago Press.

Coston, J.M. (1998). A Model and Typology of Government-NGO Relationships. *Nonprofit and Voluntary Sector Quarterly, 27*, 358-382.

Cottle, S. (2006). *Mediatized Conflict. Developments in Media and Conflict Studies*. Maidenhead, UK: Open University Press.

Cottle, S., & D. Nolan (2009). *How the media's codes and rules influence the ways NGOs work*. Retrieved from www.niemanlab.org/ngo

Dalton, B., & R. Wilson (2009). Improving quality in Australian child care. The role of the media and non-profit providers. In: D. King and G. Meagher, *Paid*

Care in Australia. Politics, profits, Practices (pp. 203-230). Sydney, Australia: Sydney University Press.

Deacon, D., & W. Monk (2000). Executive Stressed? News Reporting of Quangos in Britain. *Harvard International Journal of Press / Politics, 5*, 45-66.

Deacon, D., & W. Monk (2001a). Quangos and the Communications Dependent Society. Part of the Process or Exceptions to the Rule? *European Journal of Communication, 16*, 25-50.

Deacon, D., & W. Monk (2001b). New managerialism in the news. Media coverage of quangos in Britain. *Journal of Public Affairs, 1*, 153-166.

Deuze, M. (2002). *Journalists in the Netherlands. An analysis of the people, the issues and the (inter) national environment*. Amsterdam, Netherlands: Aksant.

Donner, P.H. (2004, May 3). *Toespraak Minister Donner n.a.v. het NVJ-onder- zoek naar de persvrijheid in Nederland.* Nederlandse Vereniging van Jour- nalisten.

Druckman, J.N. (2003). The Power of Television Images. The first Kennedy- Nixon Debate Revisited. *Journal of Politics, 65*, 559-571.

Elmelund-Præstekær, C., D.N. Hopmann, & A.S. Nørgaard (2011). Does Media- tization change MP-Media Interaction and MP Attitudes towards the Media? Evidence from a Longitudinal Study of Danish MPs. *International Journal of Press / Politics, 16*, 382-403.

Entman, R. (1989). *Democracy without Citizens. Media and the Decay of Ameri- can Politics.* New York, NY: Oxford University Press.

Entman, R. (2003). Cascading Activation. Contesting the White House's Frame After 9/11. *Political Communication, 20*, 415-432.

Eshuis, J., & E.H. Klijn (2012). *Branding in Governance and Public Manage- ment.* London, UK: Routledge.

Ester, H. (2007). The Media. In: C. Hamilton & S. Maddison, *Silencing Dissent. How the Australian government is controlling public opinion and stifling de- bate* (pp. 101-123). Crows Nest, Australia: Allen & Unwin.

Fortunati, L. (2005). Mediatization of the Net and Internetization of the Mass Media. *International Communication Gazette, 67*, 27-44.

Fowkes, L. (2009). Non-profits and the Job Network. In: P. Saunders & M. Ste- wart-Weeks, *Supping with the Devil? Government Contracts and the Non- Profit Sector* (pp. 33-39). St. Leonards, Australia: The Centre for Independent Studies.

Gandy, O.H. (1982). *Beyond Agenda Setting. Information Subsidies and Public Policy.* Norwood, Australia: Ablex.

Giddens, A. (1984). *The constitution of society. Outline of the theory of structu- ration.* Cambridge, UK: Polity Press.

157

Hajer, M. (2009). *Authoritative governance. Policy-making in the age of Mediatization.* New York, NY: Oxford University Press.

Halligan, J. (2006). The Reassertion of the Centre in a First Generation NPM System. In: T. Christensen & P. Laegreid, *Autonomy and Regulation. Coping with Agencies in the Modern State* (pp. 162-180). Cheltenham, UK: Edward Elgar.

Hamilton, C., & S. Maddison (2007). *Silencing Dissent. How the Australian government is controlling public opinion and stifling debate.* Crows Nest, Australia: Allen & Unwin.

Hardy, J. (2008). *Western Media Systems.* Oxon, UK: Routledge.

Hjarvard, S. (2008). The mediatization of Society. A theory of the media as Agents of Social and Cultural Change. *Nordicom Review, 29,* 105-134.

Hood, C. (1991). A public Management for All Seasons? *Public Administration, 69,* 3-19.

Hood, C. (2002). The Risk Game and the Blame Game. *Government and Opposition, 37,* 15-37.

Hood, C., O. Scott, O. James, G. Jones, & T. Travers (1999). *Regulation inside Government. Waste-Watchers, Quality Police, and Sleazebusters.* Oxford, UK: Oxford University Press.

Hoover, S.M. (2009). Complexities. The Case of Religious Cultures. In: K. Lundby, *Mediatization, concept, changes, consequences* (pp. 123-138). New York, NY: Peter Lang.

James, O., & S. van Thiel (2011). Structural devolution and agencification. In T. Christensen & P. Laegreid, *Ashgate Research Companion to New Public Management* (pp. 209-222). Aldershot, UK: Ashgate Publishing Ltd.

Jansson, A. (2002). The Mediatization of Consumption. Towards an analytical framework of image culture. *Journal of Consumer Culture, 2,* 5-31.

Keane, J. (2009). Monitory Democracy and Media-Saturated Societies. *Griffith Review, 27,* 79-102.

Kelly, J. (2007). Reforming Public Services in the UK. Bringing in the Third Sector. *Public Administration, 85,* 1003-1022.

Kepplinger, H. (2002). Mediatization of Politics. Theory and Data. *Journal of Communication, 52,* 972-986.

Kleinnijenhuis, J. (2003). Het publiek volgt media die de politiek volgen. In: Raad voor Maatschappelijke Ontwikkeling, *Medialogica* (pp. 151-212). Den Haag, Netherlands: SDU Uitgevers.

Klingner, D.E., J. Nalbandian, & B.S. Romzek (2002). Politics, Administration and Markets. Conflicting Expectations of Accountability. *American Review of Public Administration, 32,* 117-144.

Krotz, F. (2007). The Meta-Process of mediatization as a conceptual frame. *Global Media and Communication, 3,* 256-260.

Kunelius, R., & E. Reunanen (2011). Media in Political Power. A Parsonian View on the Differentiated Mediatization of Finnish Decision Makers. *The International Journal of Press / Politics, 17,* 56-75.

Laing, A. (2003). Marketing in the Public Sector. Towards a Typology of Public Services. *Marketing Theory, 3,* 427-445.

Lecy, J.D., & D.M. Van Slyke (2012). Nonprofit Sector Growth and Density. Testing Theories of Government Support. *Journal of Public Administration Research and Theory.* doi: 10.1093/jopart/mus010

Lijphart, A. (1969). Consociational democracy. *World Politics, 21,* 207-225.

Livingstone, S. (2009). On the mediatization of Everything. ICA Presidential Address 2008. *Journal of Communication, 59,* 1-18.

Lowe, I. (2007). The Research Community. In: C. Hamilton & S. Maddison, *Silencing Dissent. How the Australian government is controlling public opinion and stifling debate* (pp. 60-77). Crows Nest, Australia: Allen & Unwin.

Luyendijk, J. (2009). *People Like Us. Misrepresenting the Middle East.* New York, NY: Soft Skull Press.

Lyons, M. (2001). *Third sector. The contribution of nonprofit and cooperative enterprise in Australia.* Crows Nest, Australia: Allen & Unwin.

Lyons, M. (2009). *The Nonprofit Sector in Australia. A fact Sheet.* Sydney, Australia: The Centre for Social Impact.

Macintosh, A. (2007). Statutory Authorities. In: C. Hamilton & S. Maddison, *Silencing Dissent. How the Australian government is controlling public opinion and stifling debate* (pp. 148-174). Crows Nest, Australia: Allen & Unwin.

Maddison, S., & C. Hamilton (2007). Non-governmental Organizations. In: C. Hamilton & S. Maddison, *Silencing Dissent. How the Australian government is controlling public opinion and stifling debate* (pp. 78-100). Crows Nest, Australia: Allen & Unwin.

Maggetti, M. (2012). The media accountability of independent regulatory agencies. *European Political Science Review,* 1-24.

Mayhew, L. (1997). *The New Public. Professional Communication and the Means of Social Influence.* Cambridge, UK: Cambridge University Press.

Mazzoleni, G., & W. Schulz (1999). Mediatization of Politics. A Challenge for Democracy? *Political Communication, 16,* 47-261.

McChesney, R.W. (1999). *Rich Media, Poor Democracy. Communication Politics in Dubious Times.* Illinois, IL: University of Illinois Press.

McCombs, M. (2004). *Setting the Agenda. The mass media and public opinion.* Cambridge, UK: Polity Press.

McDonald, C., & G. Marston (2002). Patterns of Governance. The Curious case of Non-profit Community Services in Australia. *Social Policy & Administration, 36*, 376-391.

McKay, A., & D.L. Paletz (2004). The Presidency and the Media. In: L. Lee Kaid, *Handbook of Political Communication Research* (pp. 315-335). New Jersey, NJ: Lawrence Erlbaum.

Meckstroth, T.W. (1975). Most Different Systems and Most Similar Systems. A Study in the Logic of Comparative Inquiry. *Comparative Political Studies, 8*, 132-157.

Meer, M. van der, & J. Visser (2004). Arbeidsvoorziening. In: H. Dijstelbloem, P.L. Meurs & E.K. Schrijvers, *Maatschappelijke dienstverlening. Een onderzoek naar vijf sectoren* (pp. 183-244). Amsterdam, Netherlands: Amsterdam University Press.

Meyer, T. (2002). *Media Democracy. How the Media Colonize Politics.* Cambridge, UK: Polity Press.

Mulgan, R. (2002). Public Accountability of Provider Agencies. The Case of the Australian Centrelink. *International Review of Administrative Sciences, 68*, 45-59.

Newman, B., & R. Perloff (2004). Political Marketing. Theory, Research, and Applications. In: L.L. Kaid, *Handbook of Political Communication Research* (pp. 17-43). New Jersey, NJ: Lawrence Erlbaum.

Noordegraaf, M. (2000). *Attention! Work and Behavior of Public Managers amidst Ambiguity.* Delft, Netherlands: Eburon.

Norris, P. (1999). Blaming the Messenger? Political Communications and Turnout in EU Elections. In: H. Agné, C. van der Eijk, B. Laffan, B. Lejon, P. Norris, H. Schmitt & R. Sinnott, *Citizen Participation in European Politics* (pp. 99-116). Demokratiutredningens skrift nr 32, Statens Offentliga Utredningar 1999: 151.

Norris, P. (2013). Watchdog Journalism. In: M. Bovens, R.E. Goodin & T. Schillemans, *The Oxford Handbook of Public Accountability.* Oxford, UK: Oxford University Press. *Forthcoming.*

Patterson, T.E. (2000a). The United States. News in a Free-Market Society. In: R. Gunther & A. Mughan, *Democracy and the Media. A Comparative Perspective* (pp. 241-265). Cambridge, UK: Cambridge University Press.

Patterson, T.E. (2000b). Doing Well and Doing Good. *KSG Working Paper Series*, No. 1-001.

Pawson, R. (2002). Evidence and policy in naming and shaming. *Policy Studies, 23*, 211-230.

Peters, B.G. (2001). *The Search for Coordination and Coherence in Public Policy. Return to the Center?* Pittsburgh, PA: University of Pittsburgh.

Pollitt, C. (2003). *The essential public manager*. London, UK: Open University Press / McGraw-Hill.

Pollitt, C. (2012). *New Perspectives on Public Services. Place and Technology*. New York, NY: Oxford University Press.

Pollitt, C., & G. Bouckaert (2004). *Public Management Reform. A Comparative Analysis* (revised second edition). Oxford, UK: Oxford University Press.

Pollitt, C., C. Talbot, J. Caulfield, & A. Smullen (2004). *Agencies. How Governments Do Things through Semi Autonomous Organisations*. Basingstoke, UK: Palgrave Macmillan.

Posner, R. (2002). *Public intellectuals. A study of decline*. Cambridge, MA: Harvard University Press.

Prenger, M., L. van der Valk, F. van Vree, & L. van der Wal (2011). *Gevaarlijk spel. De verhouding tussen PR & voorlichting en journalistiek*. Diemen, Netherlands: AMB.

Raad voor Maatschappelijke Ontwikkeling (2003). *Medialogica. Over het krachtenveld tussen burgers, de media en politiek*. Advies 26. Den Haag, Netherlands: SDU Uitgevers.

Rainey, H.G. (2009). *Understanding and Managing Public Organizations*. New York, NY: John Wiley & Sons.

Raupp, J. (2005). Mediatization of Society. Consequences for organizational communication. *Communicaçao e Sociedade, 8*, 201-208.

Rawolle, S. (2005). Cross-Field effects and temporary social fields. A case study of the mediazation of recent Australian knowledge economy policies. *Journal of Education Policy, 20*, 705-725.

Rhodes, R.A.W. (1994). The Hollowing Out of the State. The Changing Nature of Public Service in Britain. *The Political Quarterly, 65*, 138-151.

Rhodes, R.A.W., J. Wanna & P. Weller (2008). Reinventing Westminster. How public executives reframe their world. *Policy & Politics, 36*, 461-479.

Roberts, A. (2005). Spin control and freedom of information. Lessons for the United Kingdom from Canada. *Public Administration, 83*, 1-23.

Salamon, L.M., & H.K. Anheier (1992). In search of the non-profit sector. I: The question of definitions. *Voluntas: International Journal of Voluntary and Nonprofit Organizations, 3*, 125-151.

Saunders, P. (2009). Supping with the Devil? Government Contracts and the Non-Profit Sector. In: P. Saunders & M. Stewart-Weeks, *Supping with the Devil? Government Contracts and the Non-Profit Sector* (pp 1-15). St Leonards, Australia: The Centre for Independent Studies.

Saunders, P., & M. Stewart-Weeks (2009). *Supping with the Devil? Government Contracts and the Non-Profit Sector*. St. Leonards, Australia: The Centre for Independent Studies.

Savage, S., & R. Tiffen (2007). Politicians, Journalists and Spin. Tangled relationships and shifting alliances. In: S. Young, *Government Communication in Australia* (pp. 79-92). Melbourne, Australia: Cambridge University Press.

Scheufele, D., & D. Tewksbury (2007). Framing, Agenda Setting, and Priming. The Evolution of Three Media Effects Models. *Journal of Communication*, *57*, 9-20.

Schillemans, T. (2007), *Verantwoording in de schaduw van de macht. Horizontale verantwoording bij zelfstandige uitvoeringsorganisaties*. The Hague, The Netherlands: Lemma.

Schillemans, T. (2010). Message control. De defensieve mediatisering van publieke organisaties in Australië en Nederland. *Bestuurskunde, 19*(1), 49-59.

Schillemans, T. (2011). Does Horizontal Accountability Work? Evaluating Potential Remedies for the Accountability Deficit of Agencies. *Administration & Society*, *43*, 387-416.

Schillemans, T., & S. van Thiel (2009). Onbekend en onbemind. Beeldvorming over zelfstandige bestuursorganen. *Bestuurswetenschappen, 63*, 53-72.

Schrott, A., & D. Spranger (2007). *Mediatization of Political Negotiations in Modern democracies. Institutional Charachteristics Matter*. Paper No 2. Zurich, Switzerland: National Centre of Competence in Research.

Schulz, W. (2004). Reconstructing mediatization as an Analytical Concept. *European Journal of Communication, 19*, 87-101.

Schuur, V. van, & J. Vis (2002). Haagse waakhonden. Politieke voorkeur, zelfbeeld en informatievergaring van parlementair journalisten. In: J. Bardoel, C. Vos, F. van Vree & H. Wijfjes, *Journalistieke cultuur in Nederland* (pp. 115-135). Amsterdam, Netherlands: Amsterdam University Press.

Schwartz, H. (1994). Small States in Big Trouble. State reorganization in Australia, Denmark, New Zealand, and Sweden in the 1980's. *World Politics, 46*, 527-555.

Scott, W.R., & G.F. Davis (2007). *Organizations and Organizing. Rational, Natural, and Open Systems Perspectives*. New Jersey, NJ: Pearson.

Sennett, R. (1998). *The Corrosion of Character: The Personal Consequences of Work in the New Capitalism*. New York: W.W. Norton.

Shergold, P. (2009). Social Enterprises and Public Policy. In: P. Saunders & M. Stewart-Weeks, *Supping with the Devil? Government Contracts and the Non-Profit Sector* (pp. 27-32). St. Leonards, Australia: The Centre for Independent Studies.

Smullen, A. (2007). *Translating agency reform. Rhetoric and culture in comparative perspective*. Nieuwegein, Netherlands: Amanda Smullen.

Snell, R. (2002). FoI and the Delivery of Diminishing Returns, or How Spin-Doctors and Journalists Have Mistreated a Volatile Reform. *The Drawing Board: an Australian Review of Public Affairs, 2*, 187-207.

Steen, M. van der, J. van der Spek, & M. van Twist (2010). *Figureren in het verhaal van de ander. Over gezagsdragers in beeld.* Den Haag, Netherlands: NSOB.

Stewart, J., & K. Walsh (1992). Change in the Management of Public Services. *Public Administration, 70*, 499-518.

Strömbäck, J. (2008). Four Phases of mediatization. An Analysis of the Mediatization of Politics. *International Journal of Press/Politics, 13*, 228-246.

Strömbäck, J. (2011). Mediatization and Perceptions of the Media's Political Influence. *Journalism Studies, 12*, 423-439.

Strömbäck, J., & D.V. Dimitrova (2011). Mediatization and Media Interventionism. A Comparative Analysis of Sweden and the United States. *The International Journal of Press/Politics, 16*, 30-49.

Thatcher, M., & A. Stone Sweet (2002). Theory and Practice of Delegation to Non-Majoritarian Institutions. *West European politics, 25*, 1-22.

Thiel, S. van (2000). *Quangocratization. Trends, causes, conséquences.* Utrecht, Netherlands: ICS.

Thiel, S. van (2006). Styles of Reform. Differences in quango creation between policy sectors in the Netherlands. *Journal of Public Policy, 26*, 115-139.

Thynne, I. (2003). Making Sense of Organizations in Public Management. A Back-to-Basics Approach. *Public Organization Review, 3*, 317-332.

Tiffen, R. (1999). Conflicts in the news. In: H. Thumber, *Media, power, professionals and policies* (pp. 190-205). New York, NY: Routledge.

Verhoest, K., P. Roness, B. Verschuere, K. Rubecksen, & M. Maccarthaigh (2010). *Autonomy and Control of State Agencies. Comparing States and Agencies.* Basingstoke, UK: Palgrave MacMillan.

Vermeer, C., C. van Montfort, & M. Abbink (2004). Rechtspersonen met een wettelijke taak. Verantwoording en toezicht. *Openbaar Bestuur, 14*, 17-19.

Vibert, F. (2007). *The Rise of the Unelected. Democracy and the New Separation of Powers.* New York, NY: Cambridge University Press.

Vuijsje, H. (2005). Sociaal-democraten en de valkuil van het goede. *Socialisme en democratie, 62*, 27-31.

Wallage Commisson (2001). *In Dienst van de Democratie.* Den Haag, Netherlands: SDU Uitgevers.

Ward, D. (2007). *Mapping the Australian PR state.* In: S. Young, *Government Communication in Australia* (pp. 3-18). Melbourne, Australia: Cambridge University Press.

Weaver, D., M. McCombs, & D.L. Shaw (2004). Agenda-Setting Research. Issues, Attributes, and Influence. In: L. Lee Kaid, *Handbook of Political Communication Research* (pp. 257-282). New Jersey, NJ: Lawrence Erlbaum.

Wettenhall, R. (2003). Exploring types of Public Sector Organizations. Past Excercises and Current Issues. *Public Organization Review, 3,* 219-245.

WRR (2004). *Proofs of good service provisions,* English translation of Report 70, Scientific Council for Government Policy, the Netherlands. Retrieved from www.wrr.nl

Yeung, K. (2005). Does the Australian Competition and Consumer Commission Engage in Trial by Media? *Law & Policy, 27,* 549-577.

Young, S. (2007). Introduction. In: S. Young, *Government Communication in Australia* (pp. xxiii-xxxiv). Melbourne, Australia: Cambridge University Press.

Appendix: Research notes

This book is based on a research project that effectively started in 2008 and ran until 2012. We have used different research methods and the data have been gathered at various times. The reason for combining different methods is the exploratory nature of the research project. The combination of approaches was expected to bring more new insights than a more focused approach with just one method. This appendix will describe and shortly explain the different research methods that have been used.

Data set 1: Trends in Media Coverage 1999-2011

Aim

To investigate long term trends in media coverage of public service providers.

Method

Quantitative content analysis.

Research technique

Newspaper articles were searched in LexisNexis and Factiva, focusing on a selection of search items, both in the 'titles' of articles as in the 'openings'.

Timing

The analysis was initially done in February-March 2009 through LexisNexis for Dutch and English organizations. The Australian organizations were added in September 2009 via Factiva. The research initially covered the 1999-2008 period and was updated for 2009-2011 in June and September 2012.

Selections

This study started out as an expanded replication study of Deacon & Monk's (2001a, b) earlier study of media coverage of British quango's. They had used a number of search items and showed how some organizations received most media attention and that the quality papers would provide most coverage of public service providers. This research has replicated the search items for the UK and used functional equivalents for the British newspapers and British service providers in the Netherlands and in Australia. In addition, a number of the larger third sector organizations were added to the analysis, on the basis of studies of the Dutch (Brandsen et al 2010) and Australian (Lyons 2001) third sector.

The selection of organizations was controlled for institutional stability over time.

Overview of newspapers

England: Daily/Sunday Telegraph, Financial Times, Guardian.
Australia: The Australian, Australian Financial Review, Sydney Morning Herald.
Netherlands: NRC Handelsblad, Financieele Dagblad, Volkskrant.

Overview of search words, incl. organizations

England

Quangocratisation; Quangocratization; Quango; Next Step Agency/ies; Executive Agency/ies; Unelected; Non-majoritarian Institution/s; Non-departmental public body/ies / ndpb; Regulator/s, Bank of England; Ofsted/ Inspector of Schools; Environment Agency; Competition Commission / CC; Office of Fair Trading / OFT; Arts Council England / Arts Council; Prison Service/ Chief Inspector of Prisons; Ofcom; Ofgas; British Nuclear Fuels/Bnfl; Health and Safety executive / hse; UK Statistics authority/ ONS; Student Loans Company / SLC; Forestry Commission; Nats / National Air Traffic Services.

Australia

Quangocratisation; Quangocratization; Quango; Executive Agency/ies; Statutory Authority/ies; Line agency/ies; Prescribed agency/ies; Non departmental public body/ies / ndpb, Reserve Bank of Australia/ RBA; National Environment Protection Council / NEPC; Australian Competition and Consumer Commission / Accc; National Competition Council / Ncc; Australia council for the Arts / Council for the arts; Crimtrac; Australian Communications and Media Authority / acma; Australian Energy Regulator / aer; Nemmco / National Electricity Market Management Company; Centrelink / Australian Fair Play Commission / Afpc; Australian Bureau of statistics / abs; Director of National Parks / national park service; Australian Taxation office /ato; Medicare; National transport commission / NCT; Food Standards Australia New Zealand / FSANZ; Australian trade commission / Austrade / Australia's Trade Promotion Organisation; Australian Institute of Criminology / AIC; Bureau of Meteorology / bom; Land & Water australia / LWA; Australian Transport Safety Bureau /atsb; Australian Research Council / arc; National Council on Education for sustainability (national council); Landcom; EnergyAustralia; Australian Rail Track Corporation /artc; Airservices Australia.

The Netherlands

ZBO; zelfstandig bestuursorgaan; zelfstandige bestuursorganisatie; verzelfstandigde organisatie; verzelfstandiging; quango; agentschap/pen; baten-lasten dienst/en, Nederlandsche Bank / DNB; Onderwijsinspectie / Inspectie van het onderwijs; VROM-inspectie; Nma/ Nederlandse Mededingingsautoriteit; Consumentenautoriteit; Raad voor Cultuur; DJI/ Dienst justitiele inrichtingen; Commissariaat voor de media / Cvdm; Energiekamer/ Dte; Gasunie; UWV / CWI; CBS / Centraal bureau voor de statistiek; informatie beheer groep / ib-groep / ibg; Belastingdienst; Nederlands vaccin instituut / Nvi; Rijkswaterstraat; Voedsel en waren autoriteit / Vwa; Economische voorlichtingsdienst / Evd; Nederlands forensisch instituut / nfi; Knmi; Rivm; Onderzoeksraad voor veiligheid; NWO; ncdo; Prorail; Sbb / Staatsbosbeheer; lvnl / luchtverkeersleiding.

Data set 2: Absolute and relative level (and personalization) of media coverage

Aim

Data set 1 provided gross overviews of the media coverage of a list of organizations and search words in a selection of quality newspapers. The more focused data set 2 additionally sought to capture all media coverage in all types of media for a selection of organizations in order to get

a) a sense of the absolute quantities of coverage,
b) to get a sense of the 'pack journalism'- quality of reporting by showing just how many stories would appear on the same news issue in all different media. In addition, the data set,
c) compares the quantity of media coverage of service providers to the quantity of media coverage of a sample of politicians, in order to assess whether service providers actually receive little or a large share of media attention, and
d) the data set related the personal appearances of an organization's CEO to the number of stories on an organization. This allows us to get a sense of the extent to which the CEOs of service providers become media personalities and, conversely, of the extent to which organizational news is personalized.

Method

Quantitative content analysis.

Research technique

All newspaper articles were searched through LexisNexis or Factiva, focusing on a selection of organizations, politicians and CEOs in all media in one year.

Timing

The Dutch service providers were analyzed via LexisNexis in August 2009. The analysis focused on the period August 2008 – July 2009 for most organizations. Some organizations were analyzed in different time periods, because of personnel changes in CEOs.

The analysis of Australian service providers was done in October 2009 via Factiva, focusing mostly on 2008, as this was just more practical, except for organizations undergoing leadership change in that year.

The analysis of Dutch politicians was done in October 2010 through LexisNexis and focused on 2008.

Selections

The analysis started with the same set of organizations that was used in data set 1. The analysis started with 56 organizations, 28 from both countries.

The analysis of Dutch politicians served as a benchmark: a standard for what constitutes 'high' and 'low' media coverage as politicians are the usual suspects in the political news. To this end, we chose to focus on all politicians – MP's, senior and junior ministers – of one of the parties in the Dutch coalition government. With this selection it was possible to find standards of newsworthiness for important and mediagenic politicians, but also for the average MP and for the invisible backbencher. There was really a choice of two parties, and – while there is no specific theoretical reason to choose any one of them – we chose to focus on the PvdA as it is more sympathetic to our personal political preferences.

For both organizations as politicians, their media coverage was analyzed using references to full names. Some people and organizations have 'difficult names'. For instance, the vice-prime minister was called 'Bos', which literally means 'forest', so the media search naturally gave many unreliable responses. We had to control for reliability and 2 Dutch service providers, 3 Australian service providers and 2 Dutch MP's had to be excluded from the results.

Dutch service providers and CEOs

Belastingdienst (Thunnissen); UWV (Linthorst), nederlandsche bank (Wellink), Onderwijsinspectie (Roeters), Vrom-inspectie (Paul), Nma (Kalbfleisch), Consumentenautoriteit (Hulshof), Dji (Wouters), Commissariaat vd media (Brakman), Energiekamer (dte) (Plug), Gasunie (Kramer), centraal bureau voor de statistiek (Van der Veen), informatie beheer groep (Spanjaard), Staatsbosbeheer (Kalden), Luchtverkeersleiding (Kroese and Riemens), Nederlands vaccin instituut (Van der Zeijst), Rijkswaterstaat (Keijts), Voedsel waren autoriteit (Kleinmeulman), EVD (de Veer), NFI (Tjin-A-Tsoi), KNMI (Brouwer), RIVM (Sprenger), Ondzoeksraad voor veiligheid (Vollenhove), NWO (de visser), Ncdo (van gennip), Schiphol (Cerfontaine), Holland casino (Flink), ProRail (Klerk).

Australian service providers and CEOs

Reserve Bank of Australia (Stevens), Australian Competition and Consumer Commission (Samuel). National competition council (Crawford or Feil), Crimtrac (Mcdevitt), Australian Communications and Media Authority (Chapman), Australian Energy Regulator (Edwell), National Electricity Market Management Company (Spaldin), Centrelink (Hogg), Australian Bureau of Statistics (Pink), National Park Service (Cochrane), Airservices Australia (Russell), Australian taxation office (D'Ascenzo), Medicare (Argall), National transport commission (Martin), Food Standards Australia New Zealand (Smith or McCutcheon), Austrade (O'Byrne), Australian Institute of Criminology (Tomison or Marks), Bureau of Meteorology (Love), Land and water australia (Robinson), Australian Transport Safety Bureau (Bills), Australian research council (Sheil), Landcom (O'Toole), EnergyAustralia (Maltabarow), Australian Rail Track Corporation (Murphy), Eight large service Providers

Dutch politicians (Labor Party)

Members of Parliament
M.I. Hamer (Mariëtte); J.R.V.A. Dijsselbloem (Jeroen); M.H.P. van Dam (Martijn); P.J.G. Tang (Paul); D.M. Samsom (Diederik); J. Tichelaar (Jacques); G.A. Verbeet (Gerdi); C.W.J.M. Roefs (Lia); J.L. Spekman (Hans); G.Ch.F.M. Depla (Staf); K. Arib (Khadija); A.J.M. Heerts (Ton); M.L. Vos (Mei Li) ; H.E. Waalkens (Harm-Evert); L.Th. Bouwmeester (Lea); A.M.C. Eijsink (Angelien); P.M.M. Heijnen (Pierre); E. van der Veen (Eelke); A.H. Kuiken (Attje) ; S. Bouchibti (Samira); J.A.W.J. Leerdam (John); P. Kalma (Paul); L. Jacobi (Lutz); M. Kraneveldt-van der Veen (Margot); A.G. Wolbert (Agnes); M. Besselink (Marianne); A.J.W. Boelhouwer (Jan); R.A. Vermeij (Roos); P.E. Smeets (Pauline)

169

(PvdA); Ch.D.M. Gill'ard (Chantal); L. Blom (Luuk) (kamerlid); A.J. Timmer (Anja) (PvdA); M.J. van Dijken (Marjo).

Junior Ministers
M. Bussemaker; A. Aboutaleb; N. Albayrak; F.C.G.M. Timmermans; F. Heemskerk; S.A.M. Dijksma; J. Klijnsma.

Senior ministers
W.J. Bos; G. ter Horst; R.H.A. Plasterk; C.P. Vogelaar; J.M. Cramer; A.G. Koenders; E.E. van der Laan.

Data set 3: full media coverage of all public service providers in one month

Aim
The first two data sets provided a sense of the level of reporting on public service providers. And although this provides insight in the trends over time (data set 1) and total numbers of stories on a selection of organizations (data set 2), they still did not provide a full overview of the total numbers of stories on service providers, both in absolute and in relative terms. To this end, this third data set was constructed. The data set focused on all stories on all public service providers in just one newspaper in just one month. This focused approach also allowed for qualitative coding of the stories, focusing on the level of negativity and the types of news frames.

This data set

a) assesses the total levels of reporting on public service providers,
b) assesses the relative share of news on service providers in all the news,
c) compares the news coverage on different organizational types and types of tasks,
d) analyzes the prominence of reporting on public service providers,
e) analyzes whether the news speaks positively, neutrally, or negatively about service providers,
f) analyzes the types of frames in which news stories on service providers are cast (but this analysis has not been used in this book), and
g) analyzes spokespersons: are spokespersons from the organization quoted? And are politicians quoted on the organizations?

Method
Qualitative and quantitative content analysis; manually and with Atlas.ti.

Research technique
The research was initially done manually, by simply going through the newspapers and scanning all stories, excluding the foreign news and culture sections. The research was then replicated with the help of two research assistants who recoded the stories (particularly for point f above). To this end we used the program atlas.ti as it allows for more systematic coding and analysis of results. The quantitative data have been taken from the first, manual coding exercise. The qualitative data from the second coding exercise. Intercoder reliability was 93%.

In total 695 articles were analyzed. In atlas.ti, 684 codes were attached to the 200 stories on service providers.

Timing

The first coding exercise was done in June and July 2009. The second coding exercise was done between November 2010 and January 2011.

Selections

The analysis focused on the left leaning quality newspaper Volkskrant.

The following search words (which have been correlated) were used:

Section of newspaper	• Lead story front page • Front page • Domestic news section • Economic news section • Commentary and opinion • Advertisement
Statutory type of organization	• Agency within broader department • Quasi autonomous public agency • Not for profit service provider
Type of task	• Direct services to citizens • Information and research activities • Regulatory duties
Spokespersons	• Organization quoted directly • Politician(s) quoted directly • Neither of the above
Tone of coverage	• Positive on organization • Neutral on organization • Negative on organization

Data set 4: Content analysis of organizational websites

Aim

To assess the extent to which the websites of public organizations cater to the needs of journalists.

Method

Quantitative and qualitative content analysis.

Research technique

Organizational websites were analyzed and sought for dimensions of 'mediatization'. Most items were 'digital' (the websites either did or did not have facts and figures sections), some items were arithmetical (the number of mouse clicks necessary to find the CEOs personal profile).

Timing

the first analysis was done in September-October 2009. It was extended with some organizations and was partially redone in January 2011.

Selections

The analysis focused on the same set of 56 organizations that was used in data sets 1 and 2.

The organizational websites were analyzed on the following items:

- Existence of organizational website as such
- Corporate information
- Corporate documentation / reports
- Non-corporate documentation / reports
- Podcasts / video's
- Facts & Figures section
- News section
- Press releases (in average annual nrs)
- Events
- Newsletter
- Rss-button
- Social media link

- Tag cloud
- 'Mediacenter'
- Direct link to media spokesperson
- CEO easily found (in average nr of mouse clicks)
- Personal information on CEO
- Website provides a photo of the CEO
- Downloadable, publishable photos

5. Elite Interviews

Aim

The interviews aimed to provide in-depth answers to our central research questions (on media pressure and the mediatization of organizational inputs, throughputs, and outputs) in the wordings and understandings of practitioners. The interviews were explicitly used in combination with focus groups and the small-N questionnaire: all three methods have their weaknesses and strengths. The combination of three techniques, focusing on the same issues and questions, has the advantage of potentially triangulating and cross-conforming findings.

Method

Semi-structured interviews.

Research technique

The semi-structured elite interviews ideally (and on average) ran for 1 hour, although some interviews lasted longer while others were shorter. All but one of the interviews were on a one-on-one basis. The interviews were recorded and later transcribed, with three exceptions where technical problems prohibited recording.

Timing

The interviews were held in waves. All 22 Australian interviews (including four general, orientating interviews), were held between September and December 2009. The first Dutch interviews were held in 2008, while the last interview was held in 2012. In addition, relevant quotes from earlier research with respondents from the same Dutch population (Schillemans 2007) were used. The total number of interviews was 40.

Selections

The respondents were primarily CEOs (19), senior strategic staff (14) or communications officers (7) from a variety of public and third sector service providers. Organizations were more or less randomly selected, based on convenience (location, accessibility, and networks), although some effort has been made to include various types of public services (see ch. 2).

6. Focus Groups

Aim

The focus groups had the same aim as the interviews (see above): generate in-depth answers to our central research questions (on media pressure and the mediatization of organizational inputs, throughputs, and outputs) in the wordings and understandings of practitioners.

Method

Moderated, semi-structured group discussions with homogeneous groups of participants representing coherent sets of organizations.

Research technique

The focus groups had a fixed format, where participants were first asked to formulate their first thoughts on the role of the media, then they filled out a small questionnaire and then a group discussion evolved that was guided by four general questions on a) media pressure, b) media as inputs, c) media in throughputs, and d) as outputs.

Timing

There have been seven focus groups. The focus groups were held in The Hague on June 16 and 18, 2009, in Adelaide on October 23, 2009, and in Sydney, on November 18, 19, 24, and 25, 2009.

Selections

Each focus group consisted of 4 to 9 representatives from coherent sets of organizations: public service providers within or outside of government departments, third sector organizations providing public services, and regulatory agencies.

In total, 42 respondents participated in the different focus groups. The focus groups primarily focused on senior, non-communications and non-executive, staff from service providers, although there were some exceptions.

7. Small-N survey

Aim

The survey was part of the focus groups. The survey covered the same questions as the focus group. The idea of the survey was first of all to countervail some of the effects of the group processes in the focus groups. The survey sometimes revealed suppressed variance among participants. It also served to provide quantitative outcomes on a four-point scale in addition to the qualitative outcomes of discussions.

Method

Questionnaire with 26 propositions on the role of the media, measured on a 4-part scale. The questionnaire was slightly adjusted each time to fit the specific group

Selections

The respondents were the participants in the focus groups and some others who were (sometimes in the final instance) unable to participate. The total number of respondents was 50.

Questions and propositions:

1   What is your age?
2   How many years have you been employed in your sector?
3   For which organization do you work?
4   What is your position?
5   Do you have direct contacts with journalists in this position?
6   Did you have direct media contacts in one of your prior commitments (or have you worked in journalism)?
7   Have you received media-training for your current job?
8   Are there rules-of-conduct with regard to the media at your organization?
9   "My policy field receives a lot of media-attention"
10 "It is important for my line of work to follow closely on what appears in the media"

11 "Media-stories often contain information that is relevant for my work"
12 "Our organizational executives are highly sensitive to media stories."
13 "Media stories often influence the things I do during a day"
14 "In meetings with internal and/or external people, there will often be references to recent media stories"
15 "Incidents in the media often influence the way I prioritize"
16 "In my perception, the media is de facto a positive watchdog for governments and the public sector"
17 "The media give a lot of attention to the organizations in our field"
18 "Media stories on our area are generally accurate"
19 "At work, we often speak negatively about the media"
20 "In my daily work, the question 'How will this be seen by the media' is always in the back of my head"
21 "It is important for organizations such as ours to avoid damage to their reputations"
22 "The central government departments that we deal with make active use of the media"
23 "The peak organizations and interest groups in our field make active use of the media"
24 "Public communication now plays a central role in internal processes"
25 "It is important in our work to be able to see reputational- and communication risks in advance"
26 "Our organization handles the media competently".